To

KATHERINE GOLDING ROSENBLATT

IN APPRECIATION OF TRUE COMRADESHIP

THIS WORK IS DEDICATED

BY HER HUSBAND

THE AUTHOR

THE CHARTIST MOVEMENT

Je ne propose rien,
je n' impose rien:
j' expose.

PREFACE

SOCIETY, like every individual, has a bias of its own:
while frequently ready to make a lasting sensation of one
social event, it is just as prone to ignore other phenomena
of no less historical importance. The study of the nature
and the causes of the social bias, in the broad sense of the
word, would be an interesting and grateful task for the so-
ciologist, while the analysis of the particular social event
must be confined, according to the nature of the latter, to a
distinct branch of the so-called Social Sciences.

The Chartist Movement is one of the tacitly ignored factors of the social evolution of the nineteenth century.
People have always spoken of the personal characteristics of
John Russell, Disraeli, or Gladstone, far more than of the
aspirations of several million men who believed in, strove
and suffered for the cause known as Chartism. By far,
more has been written of individuals like Robert Owen and
Richard Cobden than of the whole revolutionary movement
which embraced a period of more than a decade. The student, indeed, knows from his history that Chartism was a
political movement; that the Chartists fought for " six

points " which were embodied in the People's Charter. He undoubtedly knows also the funny side of the story, and, together with the writer of his history, mocks those fraudulent fellows, the Chartists, who affixed the signatures of Queen Victoria and a few other high dignitaries to the petition of almost one-fifth of the English nation. Incidentally, one meets some attestation of Chartism as " the only genuine, earnest, serious, popular movement in England since the days of the commonwealth," [1] and hears that "the story of the great social movement which is comprised in the history of Chartism is of greater importance than the disputes of the Whigs and Tories." [2] But it is a rather curious fact that, excepting Gammage's *History of the Chartist Movement*, which lays no claim to any scientific analysis of the movement and its causes, there is not a single work in the English language devoted to the subject which might satisfy the more earnest student.

The aim of this work is not only to give a fair and impartial presentation of the facts, but also to make an attempt at their interpretation and to show their interrelation. The social life of England during the first half of the last century in all its important aspects will have to be brought into the limelight. The political situation must, of course, serve as a background for the picture of a movement carried on ostensibly for political reform. But the study of none of the social and political conditions can be compared in weight with the analysis of the strictly economic state of that period. Indeed, whatever we may think of the Materialistic Conception of History as a general philosophy, there can hardly be any doubt that in all the *struggles of labor*, the " bread

---

[1] William Clarke, *Political Science Quarterly*, vol. iii, 1888, p. 555.

[2] Spencer Walpole, *History of England from the Conclusion of the Great War in 1815*, London, 1886, vol. iii, p. 500.

and fork question " is the very seed of historical causation. Regarding the Chartist Movement primarily as a labor movement and as the first compact form of class struggle, the author, therefore, deemed it necessary, after a succinct survey of the political situation, to devote the first part of his work to a careful examination of the economic condition in general and the labor condition in particular which prevailed in " Merry England " immediately before and during the period of the Chartist Movement.

The present monograph comprises only the first stages of the movement. The original intention to publish an extensive study covering the whole period could have been carried out only by going to England for the purpose of collecting additional material. This design was frustrated by the present war. It has therefore become necessary to divide the work into two volumes, the second of which, the author hopes, will appear at a later date.

In the preparation of this work, it was considered essential to guard against personal predilections and sympathies. The material was collected with care from first-hand sources; the facts were presented without any design to fit a pet theory; and the heroes of the story were allowed to introduce themselves and to play their rôles without any stage-managing on the part of the historian. It is, perhaps, on account of this impartiality and lack of prejudice that some portraits vary materially from those which have been hitherto drawn.

In conclusion, the author wishes to acknowledge his profound gratitude to Professor Edwin R. A. Seligman both for the interest he has always taken in this work and for the privilege of using his invaluable collection of Chartist literature and documents.

F. F. R.

APRIL 22, 1916.

CONTENTS

CHAPTER I

PROTOTYPES OF CHARTISM

CHAPTER II

THE WHIG RULE

CHAPTER III

The New Poor Law

CHAPTER IV

The Universal Distress

CHAPTER V

LABOR LEGISLATION AND TRADE UNIONISM

CHAPTER VI

THE PEOPLE'S CHARTER

CHAPTER VII

THE LEADERS

CONTENTS

CHAPTER VIII

THE GOSPEL OF REVOLT

CHAPTER IX

THE PEOPLE

CHAPTER X

The Petition, The Convention and The Government

CHAPTER XI

THE WRESTLING FORCES

CHAPTER XII

The Newport Riot

Appendix A

Appendix B

CHAPTER I

> Chartism means the bitter dis-
> content grown fierce and mad.
> . . . It is a new name for a
> thing which has had many
> names, which will yet have
> many.—*Carlyle*.

PROTOTYPES OF CHARTISM

THE term Chartism was coined in 1837 to designate a
set of principles which were subsequently embodied in the
famous " People's Charter ". Universal suffrage, equal
representation, annual parliaments, no property qualifications, vote by ballot, and payment to members — these
formed the " six points " which for a number of years
eclipsed all other political and social creeds. At its inauguration the movement attracted a number of recruits from
the ranks of the middle class. In time, however, Chartism
became ever more crystallized as a distinct labor struggle
for the reconstruction of society. The form of the demands were purely political, but the object was strictly
economic. Political equality was proclaimed as the only
weapon to secure equality of condition and the abolition of
class privilege. The concomitant social equality would
then pull down the mountains of wealth and fill up the
valleys of want. The task could be effected by the workingmen only. Coöperation of the middle class was generally tabooed as spelling imminent treason and danger to the
people's cause. It was this expression of class consciousness and realization of class interests that distinguished
Chartism both from utopian socialism and from previous
democratic movements in England.

Long before the Chartist demands were framed in the

People's Charter, political reform, of one kind or another, had been urged by the friends of the people. The spirit of democracy, which had been quelled by Cromwell's defeat of the Levellers, revived a century later. Indeed, some of the Chartist " points " were promulgated as early as 1769 by the " Society of the Supporters of the Bill of Rights," which, among other parliamentary reforms, demanded equal representation and annual parliaments. Petitions were for the first time presented to Parliament, protesting that its members were not self-representing individuals, but trusted delegates whose authority ceased the very moment they disregarded the wishes and interests of their constituents. Pitt, the Earl of Chatham, soon pronounced himself a convert and professed that " the constitution intended that there should be a permanent relation between the constituents and representative body of the people." On the first of May, 1771, he asserted that "the act of constituting septennial parliaments must be repealed. . . . Our whole constitution is giving way, and, therefore, with the most deliberate and solemn conviction, I declare myself a *convert to triennial parliaments*." [1] His son, William Pitt, went even further, declaring that " the restoration of the House of Commons to freedom and independency, by the interposition of the collective body of the nation, was essentially necessary to our existence as a free people "; that an equal representation of the people by annual elections and the universal right of suffrage appeared to him " so reasonable to the natural feelings of mankind, that no sophistry could elude the force of the arguments which were urged in their favor." The bills which he introduced in 1782, 1783 and 1785 provided for the extension of the franchise to householders, and for the gradual extinction of all rotten boroughs.

William Pitt was far from being an extremist among his

[1] *Chatham Correspondence*, edited by W. S. Taylor, Esq., and Captain John Henry Pringle, London, 1840, vol. iv, p. 174.

colleagues.   The writings of Stanhope and of Major John
Cartwright appeared as early as 1774 and 1776, respectively,
and demanded *universal suffrage* as a natural right.   In his
Legislative Rights of the Commonalty Vindicated, Cartwright argued that " freedom is the immediate gift of God
to all the human species," and that the franchise is a pre-
requisite of freedom.   " The very scavenger in the streets
has a better right to his vote than any peer to his coronet, or
the king himself to his crown; for the right of the peer and
of the king are derived from the laws of *men*, but the
scavenger's from the laws of God ".   This idea became so
popular that the Whigs began to consider it advantageous
to identify themselves with the reformers.   Aristocratic
clubs, such as the " Constitutional Society ", the " Whig
Club ", and the " Society of the Friends of the People ",
vied with each other in radicalism and in their emulation
of the idealistic maxims of Rousseau and the French En-
cyclopedists.   In 1780 the Duke of Richmond introduced a
bill for *universal suffrage* and *annual parliaments*.   The
preamble contended that since the life, liberty and property
of every man is or may be affected by the law of the land
in which he lives, no man is, or can be, actually represented
if he has no vote in the election of the representative whose
consent to the making of laws binds the whole community.
The state of election of members of the House of Commons
was declared as a gross deviation from the " simple and
natural principle of representation and equality."   In several places members were returned by the property of *one*
man while the number of persons who were suffered to
vote did not amount to *one-sixth* of the whole community.
The great majority of the commoners were thus governed
by laws to which they had not consented either by themselves or by their representatives.[1]   Triennial and septen-

[1] Compare this with the preamble of the " People's Charter ".   See
Appendix B.

nial Parliaments were described as tending "to make the representatives less dependent on their constituents than they always ought to be ". The same year Charles James Fox, the Whig leader and Chairman of the Committee of Westminster Electors, recommended the very same " six points " which were later embodied in the " People's Charter ". The " six points " were also urged by the " Society for Constitutional Information ", which included among its leaders a number of the most distinguished members of the English nobility, such as the Duke of Richmond, the Duke of Bedford, the Earl of Derby, the Earl of Effingham, the Earl of Selkirk, Lord Mountnorris, and others.

The bright prospects of Major Cartwright and his adherents, however, soon came to an end. The germs of radical ideas, which had infected the nobility, began to spread also among the lower strata. The alarmed government found itself in a lurch, and its peace of mind had to be bought at the price of coalition in 1783 between Lord North, the representative of the government, and Mr. Fox, the spokesman of the Whigs. This coalition brought about a complete metamorphosis in the attitude of the Whigs, which became the more intense during the French Revolution. A feeling of abhorrence swayed the professed reformers against all societies which were suspected of revolutionary ideas. All attempts at parliamentary reform were doomed to crushing defeat. The former illustrious advocate of reform, Edmund Burke, agreed in this matter with his rival Pitt. In his great zeal he stigmatized the people as a " swinish multitude ", and led the Whigs in their support of the government policy of oppression.

The adhesion to the government on the part of the aristocracy was the natural reaction of their optimistic idealism which evaporated when brought under pressure of active life. They had believed that the doctrine of " natural, un-

alienable and equal rights" could be disseminated among
the people with perfect safety to their own class and tradi-
tions. Some even went so far as to contend that "equality"
was a safeguard against "levellers". This view was eluci-
dated by the Duke of Richmond in the following extract of
his letter to Lieutenant-Colonel Sharman:

Another subject of apprehension is that the principle of allowing to every man an equal right to vote tends to *equality*
in other respects, and to *level property*. To me it seems to
have a direct contrary tendency. The equal rights of men to
security from oppression, and to the enjoyments of life and
liberty, strike me as perfectly compatible with their unequal
shares of industry, labor and genius, which are the origin of
inequality of fortunes. The equality and inequality of men
are both founded in nature; and whilst we *do not confound
the two*, and only support her establishments, we can not err.
The protection of property appears to me one of the most
essential ends of society; and so far from injuring it by this
plan, I conceive it to be the only means of preserving it; for
the present system is hastening with *great strides to a perfect
equality in universal poverty*.[1]

The French Revolution led some of the English aristocracy to realize that abstract ideas of *equality* and *natural
rights* meant absolutely nothing to the common people, unless they went hand in hand with concrete equality in distribution of wealth. Moreover, they learned that the *abstract* idea of *natural rights* was the treacherous snake that
goaded on the people to demand *concrete* equality, and they
determined to avert this at any cost. Burke's *Reflections
on the French Revolution*, published in 1790, preached a
crusade against *Republican* France, as well as against
French principles in England. The *Reflections* exerted a

---

[1] *The Right of the People to Universal Suffrage and Annual Parliaments*, August 15, 1783 (published in London, 1817).

deep influence on the men in power, but at the same time
gave an impetus to the counter activities of the radicals.
The Rights of Man by Thomas Paine, the exact antithesis
of the *Reflections*, gained a wide circulation among the
middle and lower classes. The arduous task of reform was
taken up by the " London Corresponding Society ", which
was founded by Thomas Hardy, a shoemaker. Counting
but four members at its inauguration, the first meeting in
1792 was attended by nine individuals, all personally acquainted with each other. Encouraged by the endorsement
of the Duke of Richmond, the Society jealously began to
spread its tenets all over the United Kingdom and, within
a short period, attained importance and celebrity as one of
the largest radical organizations. The government, in its
alarm, was led to believe that " there were evil-minded persons in the country, who, acting in concert with other persons in France, designed to overturn our happy constitution, and introduce a system of bloodshed and plunder."
The war with France in 1793 was primarily a war against
Jacobinism, and Pitt, who was always seeing visions of
" thousands of bandits ", was logically compelled to combat
the foe within the country. Numerous spies were employed
to shadow the steps of every suspicious person, and on the
testimony of these spies, many were subjected to severe
penalties. A certain Mr. Frost, an attorney, was sentenced
to six months' imprisonment, to stand in the pillory and be
struck off the roll, because he had dared once in a coffee-
house to declare himself " for equality and no king ". A
well-known Mr. Ridgway was sentenced to four years' imprisonment and £200 fine for selling Thomas Paine's *Rights
of Man*. The former friends of the " London Corresponding Society" began to see treason in its activities. Two delegates sent by this society to Scotland in 1793 were arrested,
tried, convicted, and transported for fourteen years. In its

report of 1794, the Secret Committee of the House of Commons claimed to have discovered seditious practices. It was this report that was chiefly responsible for the suspension of the *habeas corpus* act.[1] Pitt declared the matter urgent, and the bill was passed at a special sitting the next day after its introduction by the government. Fox openly accused the ministers of a design to terrorize the people in order to shield themselves from the condemnation for involving the country in a disastrous war. The government became inexorable in its oppression of associations, as well as of individuals. Reform bills were introduced only to encounter ignominious defeat. All reform societies were disbanded, all public meetings prohibited, and reformers were rendered innocuous either through imprisonment or intimidation. For nearly two decades the English people lived, as it were, in a state of internal siege.

Radicalism had been crushed to revive again, however, with much greater force, after the war cloud, which hovered over Europe for almost a quarter of a century, was dispersed at Waterloo. The war made England a world-monopolist. Foreign manufacturers, writhing under the sword of Damocles in their own countries, invested their capital in England which alone was safe from foreign invasion. By virtue of the complete monopoly of Great Britain as a water-carrier, English trade was carried on in the remotest parts of the world. All this changed with the end of the Napoleonic career. The demand for English manufactures suddenly shrank, capital was withdrawn, and labor thrown out of employment. The disbanded militia and discharged sailors greatly swelled the ranks of the unemployed. Symptoms of discontent which were local in the beginning, soon became universal and burst into violence after the passage of the Corn Laws in 1815. Owing to the

[1] *Cf. Address to the Nation* of 1797 by the " London Corresponding Society," in the *English Chartist Circular*, vol. ii, no. 54.

failure of the harvest and the high import duties, the price
of wheat during 1816 rose from 52s. 10d. to 103s. 7d., and
jumped still higher during the first months of 1817.[1]   To
urban riots, many of which were not suppressed without
bloodshed, and to machine-breaking were added peasant in-
surrections and incendiarism.   Flags were hoisted with
ominous mottoes, like " Bread or Blood "; " Willing to
work, but none of us to beg ".   The distress assumed
threatening proportions.   The attention of Parliament was
called to the fact that whole parishes had been deserted,
and the crowd of paupers, increasing in numbers as they
went from parish to parish, spread wider and wider this
awful desolation.

The failure on the part of the House of Commons to
alleviate the condition of the distressed revived the feeling
of hostility towards the government, and political agitators
soon emerged from obscurity.   Parliamentary reform was
again urged as the panacea for all social evils.   But this
time the demand emanated from a group of men entirely different from their predecessors, the reformers of the eighteenth century.   They came not from the ranks of aristocracy and they appealed not to aristocracy.   They were
humble writers of " two-penny trash ", and their writings
were intended for the still humbler workingmen.   The members of the radical clubs of the eighteenth century, as Burke
aptly argued against them, conceived reform not as a means
of expediency and necessity, but as a means of advancing
justice.   The later reformers cared very little for abstract
ideas; they demanded political equality as a necessary
weapon in the daily struggle for existence of the lower
classes, and their *Hampden Clubs* became the haunts of
courageous men.   The writings of William Cobbett [2] be-

---

[1] *Cf.* Thomas Tooke, *History of Prices and of the State of the Circulation from 1793 to 1837*, vol. i, London, 1838, p. 390.

[2] William Cobbett (1762-1835), one of the most prominent and bril-

came the New Testament in almost every cottage in the manufacturing districts. According to his contemporaries, Cobbett's *Political Register* was read at "meetings of people in many towns, and one copy was thus made to convey the information to scores of persons."

liant journalists of the first half of the nineteenth century and one of the most remarkable personalities, was a descendant of a humble family and the son of a laborer, who came to have "laborers under him." He could not remember the time when he did not earn his own living. In 1783 he established himself as an attorney's clerk, but before long the erratic lad began to feel himself shackled by the routine and drudgery of his office. He enlisted in the 54th Foot, and sailed to America, where he stayed with his regiment for seven years. After his discharge he went for a short time to England. There he accused three of his former officers of fraud, was courtmartialed and fled back to America. He settled in Philadelphia, where he maintained himself and his wife by teaching English to French immigrants. He founded a daily paper, which he styled the *Porcupine Gazette*, and wrote abusive articles under the pseudonym of "Peter Porcupine." He bitterly attacked the American Republic and the most popular men of the country. His journal soon brought him into trouble and he fled again, this time to his native country, in order to escape the payment of a penalty of 5,000 dollars for libel. In England he was welcomed by the Tories, and with their aid published at first the *Porcupine* and, then, in 1802, the *Register*, which led a guerilla warfare with the pillars of society, and which before long obtained the most powerful influence all over the country. The Tories became indignant with his behavior and waited for an opportunity to get square with their former protegé. For his severe attack on the government for employing German soldiers to flog English troops who participated in a mutiny, he was indicted for libel, sentenced to two years' imprisonment and fined £2,000. This sentence taught Cobbett a useful lesson of which he availed himself after his release: he learned how to advocate reforms without giving the government prosecutor a probable chance of success. From prison he emerged an extreme Radical and Revolutionist. He earnestly believed that the social evils would be remedied by political reforms and stopped short of nothing that aimed at the attainment of these reforms. As a member of Parliament, to which he was elected in 1830, he attacked the New Poor Law, and, with the exception of a few eccentricities which he displayed, as, for example, his prejudice against the Jews and his opposition to the Anti-Slavery movement, he remained till the last, as Southey called him, "an Evangelist of the populace."

In justice to Cobbett, it must be said that originally his idea was to make the people realize the want of reform and to offer constitutional guidance, " combined with firmness and temper." He hoped to inspire the masses " with patience and fortitude " and avert their sporadic outbursts of violence and machine-breaking. As to the *Hampden Clubs*, they had great faith in " the noblemen and gentlemen " of whom they were composed, and in the several hundred petitions to Parliament, asserting that in such wise they will " insure a redress of that intolerable grievance, *taxation without representation*, which has been the true cause of that universal distress which the nation now suffers." [1]

The government, however, felt great apprehension at the activities of the clubs. Their perfect organization was in itself something which could not be overlooked. The House of Commons had great cause to be alarmed at the report of its Secret Committee of the 19th of February, 1817, which portrayed the *Hampden Clubs* as disseminators of rebellion :

It appears to be part of the system of these clubs to promote an extension of clubs of the same name and nature, so widely as, if possible, to include every village in the kingdom. The leading members are active in the circulation of publications likely to promote their object. Petitions, ready prepared, have been sent down from the metropolis to all societies in the country disposed to receive them. The communication between the clubs takes place by the mission of delegates; delegates from these clubs in the country have assembled in London, and are expected to assemble again early in March. Whatever may be the real objects of these clubs in general, your Committee have no hesitation in stating, from information on which they place full reliance, that in far

[1] See the *Political Register* of Dec. 21, 1816; the *Full Report of the Proceedings of the meeting, convened by the Hampden Clubs . . . on Saturday, the 15th of June, 1816*; also Samuel Bamford, *Passages in the Life of a Radical*, London, 1844, vol. i.

the greater number of them, and particularly in those which are established in the great manufacturing districts of Lancashire, Leicestershire, Nottinghamshire, and Derbyshire, and which are composed of the lower order of artisans, nothing short of a Revolution is the object expected and avowed.

As a matter of fact, however, the *Hampden Clubs* were rather conservative in their demands and moderate in language in comparison with the "Society of Spencean Philanthropists," which was instituted in 1816 for the discussion of "subjects calculated to enlighten the human understanding." Besides their opposition to machinery and their doctrine of communism in land, these "Philanthropists" endeavored to "enlighten" the people that "it was an easy matter to upset government, if handled in a proper manner."

History repeated itself. To paraphrase the "Declaration" of the *Hampden Club,* the want of reform made the people feel, and misery made them speak. Meetings of protest against the government and the notorious riot at Spa Fields brought about the new suspension of the *habeas corpus* act. As to what this meant, the following lines of Samuel Bamford may bear witness:

The proscriptions, imprisonments, trials and banishments of 1792 were brought to our recollections by the similarity of our situation to those of the sufferers of that period. It seemed as if the sun of freedom were gone down and a rayless expanse of oppression had finally closed over us. Cobbett, in terror of imprisonment had fled to America; Sir Francis Burdett had enough to do in keeping his own arms free; Lord Cochrane was threatened, but quailed not. Hunt was still somewhat turbulent, but he was powerless. . . . Our Society became divided and dismayed; hundreds slunk home to their looms, nor cared to come out, save like owls at nightfall, when they would perhaps steal through bye-paths or behind hedges, or down some clough, to hear the news at the next cottage.[1]

[1] Samuel Bamford, *op. cit.,* vol. i, p. 44.

The suspension of open meetings was followed by the formation of various secret societies aiming at reforms which again were almost identical with those for which the Chartists subsequently fought on penalty of imprisonment or transportation. " Benefit Societies ", " Botanical Meetings ", and similar ostensibly innocent associations called for revolution as the only means for redress. The suffering masses were assured that reform would produce economy and consequently diminish taxation, which, in its turn, would enable the workingman to increase his home consumption. *Taxation without representation* again, as a few decades before, was denounced as the root of all evil. All petitions for reform were, as ever, rejected by the government. The wrath of the people, which for some time had been smoldering under the cover of secret meetings, finally broke out in 1819 in a series of defiant public demonstrations at Birmingham, Leeds, Stockport, Smithfield, and other manufacturing districts, and culminated in the Manchester Massacre of August 16, 1819. A large demonstration, estimated at about eighty thousand persons, was indiscriminately attacked by military forces. Unable to penetrate the compact mass of human beings, the cavalry plied their sabres to clear a way for the yeomanry, who dashed, wherever there was an opening, pressing, trampling and wounding hundreds of men, women and children. The massacre precipitated bitter protests from all over the land. The authorities tried in vain to minimize the real significance of the outrage by declaring it a mere accident. The working class was overwhelmed with the feelings of resentment and of revenge, which were admirably voiced by Shelley in his " Mask of Anarchy ":

> " And at length when ye complain
> With a murmur weak and vain,
> 'Tis to see the Tyrant's crew
> Ride over your wives and you—
> Blood is on the grass like dew.

> Then it is to feel revenge
> Fiercely thirsting to exchange
> Blood for blood—and wrong for wrong—
> Do not thus when ye are strong."

Protests passed into action. The agitators declared the Kingdom in a state of Civil War. The general disaffection was attributed directly to the irritation of want and economic injustice.[1] Revolt and anarchy reigned supreme in all manufacturing districts. The agitator Thistlewood found many adherents to his plan to overthrow the government. Executions for high treason became common events. But nothing could curb the awakened slave, who, together with Shelley, felt that his very life depended on "Freedom":

> " Thou art clothes, and fire, and food
> For the trampled multitude—
> No—in countries that are free
> Such starvation cannot be,
> As in England now we see."

The workingmen were taught and led to fight for " clothes, and fire, and food ", and to consecrate their very lives to the cause of *freedom*, which they confounded with universal suffrage. Mis-government was considered the source of all social evils, and the control of Parliament was, therefore, looked to as the only remedy by which the whole world might be relieved. The French Revolution of 1830 gave a fresh impetus to the popular discontent. The middle classes promptly seized this opportunity to enroll the support of the National Political Unions of workingmen to their Reform Bill. After the passage of the Reform Act of 1832 the political agitation subsided for a few years only to assume a more formidable aspect in the Chartist Movement.

[1] See Gracchus, *Letter to Lord Sidmouth on the Recent Disturbances at Manchester*, London, 1819.

CHAPTER II

THE WHIG RULE

THE fourth decade of the nineteenth century was a period of trial for the English nation and brought a series of bitter disappointments to its lower strata. To begin with, the political machinery of the Whig rule, which at its inauguration had inspired great hopes, soon fell into a state of stagnation and absolute incompetence. The people, who at the beginning of the decade were all exalted with aspirations for social justice, for equality and fraternity, saw themselves deserted and their cause betrayed by their standardbearers. The honeyed promises of the middle class, made through their representatives in the beginning of the thirties, were but the baits of politicians who turned recreant upon the achievement of their object. It became evident that their aim had been simply to wrest the power from the landed aristocracy, and to further their own interests. Their craving for political power was in accord with the economic doctrine of rent, which was promulgated by Ricardo, the first mouthpiece of the capitalist class. According to this doctrine, rent is a transfer of wealth from the capitalist to the landlord; rent and profit fluctuate, therefore, on opposite scales, —the rise in the former necessarily causing a fall in the latter. The scales were controlled by the landlords, and it became a matter of prime importance to reverse this control. The Corn Laws were a thorn in the side of the manufacturers, and all taxes were attacked as a baneful burden on industry. Sydney Smith gave expression to this sentiment in his characteristic style:

The schoolboy whips his taxed top, the beardless youth man-
ages his taxed horse with a taxed bridle on a taxed road, and
the dying Englishman, pouring his medicine which has paid
7 per cent into a spoon that has paid 15 per cent, flings himself back upon his chintz bed which has paid 22 per cent, makes
his will on an £8 stamp, and expires in the arms of an apothe-
cary who has paid a license of £100 for the privilege of putting
him to death.   His whole property is then immediately taxed
from 2 to 10 per cent.   Besides the probate, large fees are demanded for burying him in the chancel.   His virtues are handed
down to posterity on taxed marble, and he will then be gathered to his fathers to be taxed no more.

There were, indeed, few who during the fight for the
Reform Bill realized that the interest of the manufacturers
in the reform movement was actuated by selfish motives.
The organ of the radical group of the working class, the
Poor Man's Guardian, had on various occasions, in 1831 and
1832, warned the laborers that " the bill will only increase
the influence of landholders, merchants, manufacturers and
tradesmen ", and that it was the " most tyrannical, the most
infamous, the most hellish measure," as the poor " will be
starved to death by thousands if this bill pass, and thrown
on to the dunghill, or on to the ground, naked like dogs." [1]
The national Union of the Working Classes denounced the
bill as a mere expedient " to deceive the people, and no ways
calculated to better the condition of the working people."
" Orator " Hunt [2] was even more emphatic in his condemna-

[1] See "Last Warning on the Accursed Reform Bill," in the *Poor
Man's Guardian*, April 11, 1832.

[2] "Orator" Henry Hunt (1773-1835), at one time the friend of Cobbett and a member for Preston, was a Somersetshire gentleman and a
liveryman of London.   In his youth he was committed to the King's
Bench Prison for six weeks as a penalty for a duel which he had fought
with Lord Bruce.   In prison the young Tory came in contact with
some discontented persons and listened to a great deal of inflammatory

tion of the bill, root and branch, as an instrument of restriction and as an attack on the poor. But Hunt was denounced as a " demagogue " and " egotist ", while Lord John Russell, the hero of the Reform Bill, was almost universally applauded for his speech in favor of the bill. He showed the absurdity and the crying injustice of the system of election which had prevailed in England and which had allowed a " green mound " or a " stone wall, with three niches in it ", to send two members to Parliament, while large flourishing towns, full of trade and activity, containing vast magazines of wealth and manufactures had no representation.[1] The sympathies of the masses were decidedly in favor of the bill. With the exception of a small radical faction, the workingmen rallied round Thomas Attwood, the leader of the Birmingham Political Union, who, according to Francis Place,[2] was then regarded " the most influential man in England ", and who was credited with having worked the hardest to carry the Reform Bill.

The secret, however, soon leaked out that the working class had been hoodwinked. Before long the Whig leaders began to speak of their old popular allies, " the Birmingham fellows ", with affected indifference and open hostility. They hated to be reminded of the National Political Union,

talk, which decided his future activities, and he emerged a thorough radical. He was " the best mob orator of the day, as Francis Place puts it, and his uncompromising views and actions gained him the name of " demagogue " from his opponents, on the one hand, and of " champion of liberty " from the lower classes, on the other. He played an important rôle in the riots of 1816, and was usually referred to as the hero of Spa Fields and the Peterloo Massacre. His gigantic figure and carriage, as well as his histrionic manner of talking, rendered him an idol of the masses, and, while hated by the well-to-do people, he found solace in the love and devotion of the oppressed and poor.

[1] Cf. Lord John Russell's speech of the 1st of March, 1831, in Hansard's *Parliamentary Debates*, third series, vol. ii, pp. 1061-1089.

[2] Cf. infra, p. 76.

which had elevated them into power. Lord Melbourne confessed his strong opposition to " any radical measure or radical colleagues ".[1] The treachery on the part of the Whigs was the more revolting because of the false expectations they had raised:

It is painful, at this day,—testifies a contemporary reformer—to look back upon the delirium of joy which followed the success of this effort for real representation. That long, loud, universal shout of gladness which shook the earth and rose up to heaven, gave testimony to the hold which the idea had taken of the nation's heart. Wisely was it concealed from them at that moment of excitement, that they had scotched the snake only, not killed.[2]

The protest against the Act of 1832 was spontaneous on the part of real reformers. It was assailed for having opened up " a sluice gate of the most intolerable oppression ". The object of the bill was condemned together with its sponsors. " The men who made the Reform Bill were not fools; neither were the middle classes, for whom it was made. The Whigs saw, and the middle classes saw, that the effect of the bill would be to unite all *property* against all *poverty*." [3] Thomas Attwood, who had exerted the greatest influence to secure the passage of the Reform Act, declared that he regretted that he had worked for the reform which brought " troops of sycophants and time-servers " to the legislative chamber. The Whigs were stamped as a party for the dishonest, for the timid and for the unscrupulously ambitious, and their rule as the supremacy of the " hypocritical, conniving and liberty-undermining Whigs ".

---

[1] J. T. Bunce, *History of the Corporation of Birmingham*, Birmingham, 1878, vol. i, pp. 128-9.

[2] Tract published by the Complete Suffrage Union, *The Rise and Progress of the Complete Suffrage Movement*, London, 1843.

[3] Bronterre's *National Reformer*, Feb. 11, 1837.

The attitude of the radicals towards the ruling party can be seen from the characteristic picture drawn in one of the Chartist papers under the caption " What is Whiggery?" [1]

A Whig is a political shuffler, without honor, integrity, or patriotism. Dissimulation, selfishness, and baseness are his prime moving principles. In private life he is a stately despot, and a surly tyrant; cunning, hypocrisy, and falsehood are too frequently familiar to his mind, and he sometimes treats his workmen (if he has any) more like a gang of convicts than a useful band of honest, independent mechanics. If, as sometimes happens, they refuse to submit passively to his injustice and cruelty, they are persecuted and reviled, and compelled to seek refuge from his malignancy beyond the limits of his arbitrary authority. . . . When the Whig is a mighty politician, he courts public favor, smiles graciously on the people, makes glorious promises of reform, cajoles and flatters them, until he gets them to assist him in advancing his selfish schemes. But he treats them with ingratitude and contempt, when they afterwards remind him of his obligations and request him to perform them.

The commissions of inquiry became a byword of political corruption and inactivity:

Set them to make a report on any public subject, give them, for example, a brief to fill up against the poor and the Poor Laws, and they will do it to their employer's satisfaction; it is their vocation faithfully to serve those by whom they are paid, or hope to be paid, and little of conscientious responsibility to truth or justice is felt in the execution of the appointed task.[2]

The rampant political favoritism was also strikingly satirized by Sydney Smith, when he said that if you met a Whig,

<hr />

[1] *The Chartist Circular*, May 2, 1840.

[2] *The Black Book: An Exposition of Abuses in Church and State, Courts of Law, etc.*, London, 1835, appendix, p. 61.

whom you had never seen before, your doubt was " not whether he was a commissioner or not, but what the department of human life might be into which he had been appointed to inquire ". The hero of the Reform Bill, Russell himself, who in 1831 accused the landlords of usurpation of power in violation of the Constitution of the country, according to which " no man could be taxed for the support of the State who had not consented, by himself or his representative, to such tax ", soon became an accomplice to such usurpation, derided the demand for universal suffrage and went down in history with the well-deserved nickname of " Finality Jack ".[1]

The Whigs became even more unpopular after their election in 1835. They had come in on promise of retrenchment and, instead, they increased taxation; they had vowed reforms and, when in power, forced upon the people the odious New Poor Law. The assertion that " Whigs and Tories are the two thieves between which this nation has been crucified "[2] was not the conviction of but one individual. The Reformed Parliament discussed everything except what Carlyle styled " the alpha and omega of all questions ",—" the condition-of-England question ". The reformers were satisfied, as the bard Praed puts it:

> To promise, pause, prepare, postpone,
> And end by letting things alone.
> In short, to earn the people's pay,
> By doing nothing every day.

The ruling party was detested not alone by the radicals. Ex-Chancellor Lord Brougham, who despised the latter,

[1] The nickname was derived from a phrase of his speech of June 23, 1837, in which he referred to the Reform Bill as a " *final measure.*"

[2] See R. W. C. Taylor, *Notes of a Tour in the Manufacturing Districts of Lancashire*, London, 1842, p. 271.

expressed the sentiment of many a conservative when he said in 1839: " I have little thought to have lived to hear it said by the Whigs of 1839, ' Let us rally round the queen; never mind the House of Commons; never mind measures; throw principles to the dogs; leave pledges unredeemed; but, for God's sake, rally round the throne '." Disraeli also laid great stress on the irresponsibility of the Whigs, although he exaggerated the significance of the political causes in the Chartist movement.[1]

The Whigs were crushed by their own incompetence and treachery even as early as 1838. The notorious " Bedchamber Plot ", which brought down a tempest of ridicule on the heads of the chivalrous Whigs, gave them a chance for shelter " behind the women's petticoats ", but only for a short time. The people, disgusted with their perfidy, lost all confidence in them and overwhelmingly defeated them at the next election. Their rule, however, was the more ignominious because of the great economic distress and physical and moral degeneration which prevailed during their administration without any serious attempt being made by the government at alleviation. Indeed, so appalling was the wretchedness as to be almost beyond credence, were it not for official records of that period. This wretchedness was, to a great extent, the direct result of the New Poor Law of 1834 and its administration by the Whigs.

The chicanery and bribery on the part of the landlords, and the fraud and perjury on the part of the paupers, fostered by the old Poor Laws, made their repeal imperative. The industrial, as well as the agricultural districts, were turned into headquarters of permanent pauperism with all its revolting consequences. Riots, incendiarism, assault and murder became common events. Under these

[1] See Hansard's *Parliamentary Debates*, third series, 1839, vol. xlix, pp. 246-251.

laws the able-bodied and efficient pauper was denied the right of voluntary choice of settlement. The kind of work and his income were fixed by the magistrates, who could very seldom ascertain the man's previous earnings. The parish authorities were demoralized to the very marrow and looked upon the parish as upon their prey. The pauper had to be satisfied not only with the master they had chosen for him, but also with the woman they had made him marry.

The injudicious provisions and application of the old laws put a premium on laziness and pauperized not only indigent men, but also the respectable classes of mechanics:

I am every week astonished by seeing persons come whom I never thought would have come,—reports Mr. Chadwick, one of the Poor Law Commissioners.—The greater number of our out-door paupers are worthless people; but still the number of decent people who ought to have made provision for themselves, and who come, is very great and increasing. One brings another; one member of a family brings the rest of a family. . . . Thus we have pauper father, pauper wife, pauper son, and pauper grand-children frequently applying on the same relief-day. . . . Indeed, the malady of pauperism has not only got amongst respectable mechanics, but we find even persons who may be considered of the middle classes, such as petty masters, small master bricklayers.[1]

The bulky volumes of the Report of the Commission, of which Nassau Senior was a member, proved quite conclusively that the very foundation of English economic life was in jeopardy. Since every employer could choose between a workman solely dependent on his wages and a pauper, whose earnings were supplemented by the parish rates, it was but natural that only the latter should get employment, thus dragging down wages and increasing the

[1] *Reports from Commissioners*, 1834, vol. xxvii, p. 26.

army of professional paupers. " The surplus labourer is driven by the overseer into the market to compete with the regular workman,"—writes an investigator,—"his work is offered at a reduced price, or he is even billeted, and his pay entirely derived from the rates. With this cheap laborer the regular one can stand no chance; he is undersold in his own market, and his only property, the work of his hands and the sweat of his brows, is wrested from him ".[1] Furthermore, the Report of the Poor Law Commissioners shows that a more or less self-respecting and industrious laborer, who had managed to lay by a part of his wages for a rainy day, was refused work, " till his savings were gone; and the knowledge that this would be the case, acted as a preventive against savings ". Pauperism which reached a menacing point in 1832, when one person out of every seven was receiving relief, put the very life of the nation at stake, and became most destructive of the family and of society.[2] The repeal of the old laws was urgent also because the growth of industry and the development of the factory system needed complete mobility of labor, which the law of settlement made impossible.[3] Something had to be done, some remedy had to be found, and the reforms of 1834 were proclaimed the panacea for the social evil. The chief ingredient of the remedy has since become known as the *workhouse test*. All relief, either in money or in provisions to *able-bodied* persons, was declared illegal except when rendered in public and well-regulated workhouses, or, as the poor classes called them, " Poor Law Bastiles ".

[1] William Day, *An Inquiry into the Poor Laws and Surplus Labor, and their Mutual Reaction*, London, 1832, p. 16.

[2] See *Report from Commissioners*, 1834, vol. xxvii, pp. 45 and 54.

[3] See in this connection the *Extracts from Information received by Her Majesty's Commissioners, as to the Administration and Operation of the Poor Laws*, London, 1833, pp. 271-272.

The sudden change caused by the New Poor Law, which was strenuously opposed, among other representatives, by the friend of the poor, William Cobbett, and by the then young and uninfluential politician Disraeli, naturally intensified the hatred of the poor toward the property-owners and still more opened the eyes of the working classes to the fathomless gulf between themselves and the Liberals, into whose hands they had unsuspectingly put the reins of authority. When the bill was still pending, the uncompromising Cobbett emphatically declared that the object of the bill was " to rob the poor man to enrich the landowner ",[1] and this opinion became current all over the vast stretches of the misery-infested land. The glove which was cast to the non-possessing classes, challenging them indiscriminately either to become prisoners or to starve, was picked up with threatening air, first, in the House of Commons, by a few friends of the people, and then by the people themselves. Representative Leech warned the House that the new law would inevitably render the breach between the rich and the poor wider than it had hitherto ever been,[2] while representative Hodges prophesied trouble with the unemployed laborers. " To be sure, the discontented might be put down if they were in the wrong ", he said; " but when they had justice on their side, and were goaded on by their grievances, the recollection of any collision between them and the police or soldiery to put them down would be never effaced from their minds ".[3] Still more threatening was the speech of Thomas Attwood in the House of Commons on the 11th of August, 1834:

The people had a right to claim relief if they did not obtain

[1] Hansard's *Parliamentary Debates*, vol. xxiv, 1834, p. 1051.

[2] *Ibid.*, pp. 1059-1060.

[3] *Ibid.*, p. 1030.

employment,—as good a right as the noble Lord had to the
hat on his head. If the people were prevented from living
honestly, they would be justified in living dishonestly. . . . For
the law said, and it was a principle of our Constitution, that
obedience was to be contingent upon protection, and that where
no protection was given no obedience could be exacted.[1]

The indignation with the New Poor Law grew apace because of the stringency of administration which provoked
Mr. Harvey, representative for Southwark, to stigmatize
the new law as " one of the most cruel, heartless, and selfish bills that ever was passed into a law ", and to declare
that the funds " were administered with the most barbarous
and heartless severity ". Another representative called it
the New Poor Law Murder Bill. Daniel O'Connell, the
famous Irish patriot, was so much impressed by the accounts of the sufferings endured by the poor through the
New Poor Law that he concluded that the alleged remedy
was worse than the disease, and vigorously, though vainly,
fought its introduction in Ireland.

An amendment of the old Poor Laws was inevitable,
but the precipitate break with the established system
could not but entail disastrous results. The Poor Law
Commissioners, then known under the nicknames of
" bashaws of Somerset House " and " concentrated icicles ",
were apparently so dejected by the evils of an institution which threatened degeneracy to the whole nation,
that they could not avoid the unhappy but common
mistake of substituting one extreme for another. Representative Robinson was perfectly right, when he attacked
the third reading of the bill on the ground that the " odious
and cruel measure " contained no single feature which held
out the least prospect or hope to the poor, no single provi-

[1] Hansard's *Parliamentary Debates*, vol. xxv, p. 1224.

sion which would give additional employment to the destitute, and that it treated all able-bodied laborers alike. The
poor man, he argued, would be told, " you must either go
into the workhouse or we cannot give you relief ", and the
effect of such a system, which made no distinction whatever
between honesty and immorality, between the imbecile and
the able-bodied, would be perilous.[1]   These voices of warning, however, fell on deaf ears. The bill was passed under
protest,[2] and hardly had the people time to realize what had
taken place in the Houses, when the local " Dogberries "
began to treat them with barbarous cruelty. The discipline
which was at once introduced in the workhouses fell like a
thunderbolt on many a wretched family. Aged men found
themselves separated from their wives and imprisoned in
the workhouse, where the inmate was never allowed to
forget that he was under strict orders, and where he was
compelled to live on a diet frequently insufficient for the

[1] Hansard's *Parliamentary Debates*, vol. xxiv, 1834, p. 1042.

[2] The protest which was entered by some members of the House of
Lords against the passing of the Poor Laws' Amendment Bill contained, among others, the following reasons:

" 1. Because this Bill is unjust and cruel to the poor. It imprisons
in workhouses, for not working, those who cannot, by the hardest
labor, obtain wages sufficient to provide necessaries for their wives
and children, although the want of employment and the low rate of
wages have been occasioned by the impolicy and negligence of the
Government. . . .

" 4. Because we think the system suggested in the Bill, of consoli-
dating immensely extensive unions of parishes, and establishing workhouses necessarily at great distances from many parishes, and thereby
dividing families and removing children from their parents, merely because they are poor, will be found justly abhorrent to the best feelings
of the general population of the country; and especially inasmuch as it
introduces the children of the agricultural poor to town poorhouses,
it will conduce greatly to the contamination of their moral principles,
and be calculated to prevent their obtaining in youth those habits of
industry most likely to be beneficial to them in after-life."

See *ibid.*, vol. xxv, 1834, pp. 1098-9.

bare sustenance of life. Mothers were dragged away, like criminals, from their infants; sick men and women were made to walk long distances for relief, some of them expiring on the way. Tears and starvation became the poor man's lot.[1] The unfortunate inmates of the poorhouses were even denied the consolation of religion, being deprived of the liberty of attending houses of worship.

Such were the reforms introduced during the Whig rule.

[1] The literature of the day became permeated with expressions of indignation, of which the following lines by Maurice Harcourt, written in 1837, may serve as an example:

> "Tears! Tears are the portion of the Poor,
> For the great ones fain would see how much they can endure;
> And to prove *their* pity never fails,
> They have built the wretched union gaols,
> Where King Starvation reigns supreme,
> And plenty is a pauper's dream!
> And 'mid this mockery of life
> Lingers the pale yet lovely wife,
> Torn from her first and dearest tye,
> In this abode of gloom to die."

CHAPTER III

Oh ! glorious was that mortal's skill,
Who first devised the Poor Law Bill,
To teach in this enlightened time,
That poverty's the vilest crime.
—*Maurice Harcourt.*

THE NEW POOR LAW

THE philosophy of the New Poor Law, borrowed from James Mill, was based on the Malthusian economic doctrine. To aid the people who did not reserve seats at nature's feast meant to injure others who had better claims. The commissioners who were entrusted with the enforcement of the New Poor Law thoroughly understood their mission which was once stated by Dr. Kay at a public meeting. He said bluntly : " Our intention is to make the workhouses as like prisons as possible, and to make them as uncomfortable as possible." [1] These intentions were, indeed, carried into effect with a faithfulness worthy of a better object. The impression made by the description of the poorhouses is appalling, and even Mr. T. W. Fowle, the ardent advocate of the New Poor Law, vainly tries to conceal his confusion in an array of words, and the following lines sound like mockery : " Wise men will note with satisfaction that the use of the rod is not forbidden in the case of naughty boys. . . . The privilege of flogging enjoyed by children of the upper classes is denied to paupers above the age of fourteen." [2] The description given by Mr. Fowle of the effect

[1] Hansard, vol. xli, p. 1014.

[2] T. W. Fowle, *The Poor Law, London*, 1881, p. 139.

of promiscuous aggregation on the poorhouse inmates and especially on the children, restrained as it is, presents a lurid picture of mental and moral contamination.[1] The criminal negligence of children, who were maintained in the workhouses, on the part of the officers was exposed by a surgeon in his letter to Lord John Russell.[2] Emaciation was evident in almost all the eighty children within the walls of the workhouse of St. James:

The picture is almost too horrible to describe. I found the children with large heads, tumefied bodies, shrivelled and wasted limbs mostly in a sitting posture, with their legs crossed —and I found upon enquiring of the nurse . . . that any change from this position occasioned them pain, and caused them to cry. . . . They have, in short, become rickety from the want of exercise and, I fear, an insufficient supply of wholesome nourishment. . . . Languid and feeble circulation, and other marks of general debility, are strikingly apparent. . . . The sight was truly appalling. . . . It is quite clear that such an uniform character of disease among so many children, the offspring of different parents, must be the result of the particular manner in which these children have been nursed and maintained. . . . They are unfortunately too young to tell their own tale; but although their intellects are not sufficiently matured to give this information, their appearance and condition bespeak it but too powerfully. I do not hesitate to declare my firm belief that their wretched condition is the result of either an insufficient supply of food, or a supply of improper food, and a want of exercise. . . . Either of these

[1] Fowle, *op. cit.*, pp. 142-144. See also on this point Sidney and Beatrice Webb, *The Break-Up of the Poor Law: Being Part One of the Minority Report of the Poor Law Commission*, London, 1909, chap. 1.

[2] On the punishment and treatment of children by the workhouse authorities, see also speech of representative Ferrand in Hansard, *op. cit.*, third series, vol. lxvi, pp. 1226-1228.

causes, or the combination of them, is adequate to the production of the effects it has been my unhappiness to witness.[1]

The cruelties perpetrated in various workhouses were divulged by non-partisan men, such as the Rev. William Carus Wilson, who submitted to the legislature his report on the "wanton cruelty of the officers of the New Poor Laws."[2] These official statements and the accounts given by the *London Times* and many local opposition newspapers of the crimes committed by workhouse officials, together with the imaginative pathetic pictures of Oliver Twist and other workhouse heroes of fiction, did not fail to provoke universal detestation of the new system of poor relief. The indigent actually shrank with fear at the thought of the workhouse, and in many cases preferred to starve rather than enter the "Bastiles." The net result was that

as a matter of fact (the large towns excepted) they (the workhouses) do not contain in many cases half, in some not a quarter of the inmates for which they were built, so that the waste in keeping up large unfilled establishments, each with an expensive staff of officers, is very great, indeed; *thus the salaries and rations of officers* (including, however, that proportion which is spent in the administration of out-relief) *is considerable over a million, while the total maintenance of indoor paupers is only about a million and three-quarters.*[3]

The defenders of the New Poor Law did anything but enlighten the non-possessing classes on the real significance and desirability of the new measure. In his long and ela-

---

[1] T. J. Pettigrew, *A Letter to the Right Hon. Lord John Russell, on the Condition of the Pauper Children of St. James, Westminster*, London, 1836, pp. 11-12.

[2] William Carus Wilson, *Remarks on Certain Operations of the New Poor Laws*, Kirkby Lonsdale, 1838.

[3] Fowle, *op. cit.*, p. 141.

borate speech which he delivered in the House of Lords on July 21, 1834, the Chancellor Lord Brougham, the father of the Bill, extolled the wisdom of Malthus and declared with brutal frankness that the New Poor Law was intended as a preventive check on the unlimited increase of population.[1] This declaration, coupled with his express hatred of charitable institutions and his cynical denunciation of hospitals for old age, called forth a storm of indignation. As ever, the undaunted Cobbett came out with a characteristic reply: " The great object of the Bill," said he,

was to teach the poor to live as man and wife, without having any children. This was a base and filthy philosophy, and yet a book had been published showing the means of carrying the principles of Malthus into effect. Every farmer knew that the effect of the Bill was to take away the poor rates from the poor, and to put them into the pockets of the landlords.[2]

Cobbett's erroneous view that the Poor Law was enacted for the benefit of the landlords was shared by many of his radical colleagues. Their hatred of the landed aristocracy rendered them utterly incapable of realizing the importance and the advance of the new capitalist class. It was Bronterre, subsequently the " school-master " of Chartism, who attacked the new law as an instrument of exploitation by the manufacturers. In the first number of his *National Reformer*, dated January 7, 1837, he writes:

Our work-people, both agricultural and manufacturing, are already ground down as low as commercial avarice can grind them, without exterminating them altogether; yet the *money-monster* is not half satisfied. As a last resource, this *monster* has now passed a New Poor Law Act, to make the laborers

[1] Hansard, *op. cit.*, vol. xxv, 1834, pp. 211-251.
[2] *Ibid.*, p. 1216.

live on *coarser food*, or on no food at all—an Act which treats
the victims it has impoverished as other states treat convicted
felons—an act which gives a felon's garb, a felon's fare, and
a felon's gaol to the broken-down man whose toil has enriched the *monster*, and whose only crime is that he did not
strangle the *monster* a century ago. . . . Yes, my friends, the
New Poor Law Act is the last rotten blood-stained prop by
which the *money-monster* hopes to sustain the tottering fabric
of his cannibal system—of that merciless system, which first
makes you poor in the midst of wealth of your own producing,
and would then bastile and starve you for the fruits of its
own barbarity.

This view was subsequently elaborated by most of the
Chartist writers. Feargus O'Connor, the foremost Chartist
leader, attacked the new law on the ground that it was both
a result and a cause of the excessive use of machinery:

This act was framed by Lord Brougham, as the champion of
the middle classes, who were most strongly represented by the
steam producers, and it was framed purposely with a view to
seduce those into a delusive market who would have risen in
their might and annihilated any government that dared thus
violate their trust by the commission of wholesale plunder, had
it not been for the safe retreat promised to the abandoned in
the artificial market. It is the nature of man to use all means
to better his situation, and the poor countryman who gave up
his house and home under the compulsion of the *Poor Law
Amendment Act*, in the hope of going to a permanent situation,
was unconscious in the "hey-day" of manual labor, as then
applied to infant machinery, that each improvement in the one
would be a nail in the coffin of the other. Estates were cleared
of willing immigrants seduced by the *spirit* of the moment,
and when anticipation had failed, they then framed the stringent rules under which the hellish law had placed them, when
they sought for an asylum in the parish of their fathers. Had
it not been for machinery, the *Poor Law Amendment Act*

never would have passed—nay, never would have been ventured
upon, because the whole force of popular indignation would
have been directed against the general plunder, while opposition
was much mitigated in consequence of the casual provision
which machinery offered as a substitute; thus has the *Poor
Law Amendment Act* been another direct effect upon machinery.[1]

From the point of view of social causation, it is, indeed,
utterly irrelevant whether or not the advocacy of the New
Poor Law was prompted by personal or by class interests.
It must be conceded that, whatever the motives might have
been, the object of checking poverty and moral degradation
was commendable. The fundamental propositions of Lord
Brougham were mere truisms, " that men should be paid
according to the work they do "; that men should be employed and paid " according to the demand for their labor
and its value to the employer," and that " they who toil
should not live worse than those who are idle." [2] However,
when one puts himself in the position of the poor contemporaries of the Lord Chancellor who, directly or indirectly,
were concerned in, and affected by, the new law, he must assume a different attitude. Blinded by his extreme hatred of
charity,—even assuming that this hatred was nurtured not
by a bad heart, but by sentiments of a public-spirited man [3]
—the noble Lord displayed his feeling in a way which the
common people could not help but abhor. It must have
been brazen-headedness, if not hard-heartedness, to come before one army of destitute men and women who were dis-

---

[1] *English Chartist Circular*, no. 64.

[2] Hansard, *op. cit.*, vol. xxv, 1834, p. 218.

[3] The Lord Chancellor was apparently afraid of passing into history
with the reputation of a hard-hearted and short-sighted man, and
grasped the opportunity at the next discussion to correct this impression. See Hansard, vol. xxv, p. 436.

placed, like so many useless tools, by the new machinery,
and before another still greater army of men who were
compelled by the order of the land to shun decency and
regard thrift and savings as a thing for which they would
be punished by the parish with unemployment,—it must
have been fanatical blindness to come before the nation
with an argument like the following:

Sickness is a thing which a provident man should look forward
to, and provide against, as part of the ordinary ills of life.
. . . But when I come to hospitals for old age—as old age is
before all men—as every man is every day approaching nearer
to that goal—all prudent men of independent spirit will, in the
vigour of their days, lay by sufficient to maintain them, when
age shall end their labor.   Hospitals, therefore, for the support
of old men and old women, may, strictly speaking, be regarded
as injurious in their effects upon the community.[1]

This speech brought forth an outburst of disgust and antagonism, and was made most use of by the Tories as well
as the Radicals.

The sponsors of the New Poor Law, however, treated
with cruel disregard all the protests and warnings of their
fellow members of Parliament and other antagonists.   Far
from heeding the petitions of the people, they rejoiced at the
result achieved immediately after the enforcement of the
new provisions.   The idea of the framers of the bill, which,
to use Cobbett's words, was meant " as a stepping stone to a
total abolition of all relief for the poor",[2] seemed to approach
realization, inasmuch as both the number of applicants for
relief and the amount of relief itself were at once con-
siderably reduced.   It is true that the relief officers had to
quell many a riot in the new unions; but this little dampened

---

[1] Hansard, *op. cit.*, vol. xxv, 1834, pp. 221-222.
[2] *Ibid.*, vol. xxv, 1834, p. 1216.

the hopes of the commissioners, since the suppression was not a difficult task.[1] The *stepping-stone* proved to be of great avail, as the reduction of the poor rates in thirteen of the largest parishes reached twenty per cent the first year.[2] The expenditures for poor relief were fast sliding downward, as may be seen from the following table:[3]

RELIEF OF THE POOR

Year.	Pounds.
1832	7,036,968
1833	6,790,799
1834	6,317,255
1835	5,526,416
1836	4,717,629
1837	4,044,741

The commissioners, of course, could not deny that the progress of the change had been highly favored by the prosperous state of the manufacturing districts and especially by the cheapness of provisions which marked the first half of the decade.[4] Yet they had great faith in a system which was shunned by the people from the very start. In the Faringdon Union alone, for example, workhouse relief was offered to 240 able-bodied laborers, of whom not more than twenty entered the house, and not more than one-half of the latter remained there longer than a few days.[5]

These were good signs for the friends of the New Poor Law, and, to use Carlyle's sarcastic comments on the Reports of the Poor Law Commissioners, "a pleasure to the friend of humanity".

[1] See *First Annual Report of the Poor Law Commissioners for England and Wales*, 1835, pp. 35-36.

[2] *Ibid.*, p. 26.

[3] See *Third Annual Report of the Poor Law Commissioners, etc.*, 1837.

[4] See *Second Report of the Poor Law Commissioners, etc.*, 1836, p. 33.

[5] See *First Annual Report of the Poor Law Commissioners, etc.*, p. 27.

One sole recipe seems to have been needful for the woes of England: "refusal of out-door relief". England lay in sick discontent, writhing powerless on its fever-bed, dark, nigh desperate, in wastefulness, want, improvidence and eating care, till like Hyperion down the eastern steeps, the Poor Law Commissioners arose, and said, Let there be workhouses, and bread of affliction and water of affliction there! It was a simple invention; as all truly great inventions are. And see, in any quarter, instantly as the walls of the workhouse arise, misery and necessity fly away, out of sight,—out of being, as is fondly hoped—and dissolve into the inane; industry, frugality, fertility, rise of wages; peace on earth and good will towards men do, — in the Poor Law Commissioners' Reports, — infallibly, rapidly or not so rapidly, to the joy of all parties, supervene.[1]

The effects of the new measure were more or less disguised by the general condition of prosperity. Before long, however, they emerged to the surface. The crisis of 1836 and the series of bad harvests that followed it ushered in a period of the most abject misery. The notorious Irish famine and the distress in the highlands (Scotland) could not but augment the universal penury. After the crop of 1836 had been entirely cut off, the inhabitants of the highlands and the islands were left without potatoes, their staple article of food, almost at the beginning of winter. The grain crops could not ripen because of the general wetness of the soil, while those which partially did ripen were destroyed by the severe autumn gales and were rendered entirely useless even for the cattle. It was reported, with the fear of being rather " under the mark than of overshooting it ", that two-thirds of the population " are now, or will be long before the commencement of the next crop, without a supply of either kind of food at home, and will have to look to foreign sources to

[1] Thomas Carlyle, *Chartism*, London, 1840, p. 16.

prevent starvation." [1]   The official report of the Agent-General for Emigration, dated July 29, 1837, stated explicitly that, owing to the decline of the fisheries and the breaking up of the kelp trade, by which the bulk of the population lived, the majority of the people had become "a clear superfluity in the country." [2]

This superfluity of human beings had to emigrate from their native places in order to avoid starvation.   Ireland, in the judgment of the commissioners of 1836, was one great lazarhouse, and the Irish poor crossed over in crowds to England, congested every large town, or rambled over the country, offering their services on any terms which might induce manufacturer or farmer to employ them.   Emigration also became a prominent feature among the English peasantry.   Man hunted for a refuge from the lurking enemy—hunger. Goaded on by the illusion that clings to distant places, people abandoned their hovels and turned nomads.   The characteristic attributed by Adam Smith to man as being "of all sorts of luggage the most difficult to be transported," which was strikingly true even as late as 1837, changed, as if by magic, under the severe economic pressure of the subsequent year.   In his report to the Secretary of State for the Colonies, the Agent-General for Emigration from the United Kingdom relates that Dr. Galloway had to travel over a considerable part of Wiltshire, Dorsetshire, Hampshire, and the eastern part of Sussex, in order to secure a sufficient number of passengers for a small public

[1] *Distress in the Highlands* (Scotland). A letter addressed to Mr. Fox Maule by Mr. Robert Graham, and communicated by Lord John Russell's direction to the Commissioners of Her Majesty's Treasury. London, 1837; pp. 1-2.

[2] *Report of the Agent-General for Emigration on Applicability of Emigration to Relieve Distress in the Highlands*, dated July 29, 1837, London, 1841, p. 1.

vessel which sailed in June, 1837. In the autumn of the same year a vessel was allotted to the county of Norfolk, but the whole party, with the exception of only three families, changed their minds at the last moment. Circumstances were much changed in 1838. The government agents found no difficulty whatsoever in filling four ships from the county of Kent alone, and many applicants had to be rejected for want of room.[1] Emigration filled all channels and especially those leading to the industrial centres, which before long inevitably became infested with the most noisome quarters.

In the very center of Glasgow,—writes the superintendent of the police of that city,—there is an accumulated mass of squalid wretchedness. . . . There is concentrated everything that is wretched, dissolute, loathsome and pestilential. These places are filled by a population of many thousands of miserable creatures. The houses in which they live are unfit even for sties . . . dunghills lie in the vicinity of the dwellings; and from the extremely defective sewerages, filth of every kind constantly accumulates.[2]

In 1837 one-tenth of the Manchester and one-seventh of the Liverpool population lived in cellars, and most of them in courts with only one outlet.[3] In Bury, the population of which was 20,000, the dwellings of 3,000 families of workingmen were visited. In 773 of these dwellings the families slept three and four in one bed; in sixty-seven, five and six slept in one bed, and in fifteen one bed accommodated six and seven persons.[4] In Bolton there

---

[1] *Report to the Secretary of State for the Colonies, from the Agent-General for Emigration from the United Kingdom*, 1838, p. 6.

[2] Hansard, *op. cit.*, 1843, vol. lxvii, p. 69.

[3] *Ibid.*, 1838, vol. xxxix, p. 383.

[4] *Ibid.*, 1840, vol. li, p. 1226.

were, in 1840, 1,126 houses untenanted. In one case, seventeen persons were found in a dwelling about five yards square. In another, eight persons, two pairs of looms and two beds were found in a cellar, four by five yards, and six feet under the ground.[1] In Rochdale, five-sixths of the population had scarcely a blanket among them.[2] The chief commissioner of the police force in Manchester stated that in one room, totally destitute of furniture, three men and two women were found lying on the floor, without straw, and with bricks for their pillows. The stipendiary magistrate of the Thames Police Office reported similar observations. The descriptions of dwelling houses "with broken panes in every window-frame, and filth and vermin in every nook, with walls black with the smoke of foul chimneys, with corded bed-stocks for beds, without water,"[3] appears less shocking in comparison with the statements made by other witnesses. The dwellings in the rural districts were even worse than those in the cities. In one place a father, mother, married daughter with her husband, a blind boy of sixteen, a baby, and two girls, all occupied one room.[4] In another place a man of about sixty years of age was found living in a cow stable, without windows, floor, or ceiling, where the rain dripped through the rotten roof, and dung-heaps lay near his door.

---

[1] Hansard, *op. cit.*, vol. lviii, pp. 31-32.

[2] *Ibid.*, vol. lix, p. 635.

[3] *Report on the Sanitary Condition of the Laboring Population of Great Britain*, London, 1842, pp. 133-135.

[4] Hansard, vol. lxxiii, pp. 882-884.

CHAPTER IV

Child, is thy father dead?—
    Father is gone:
Why did they tax his bread?—
    God's will be done.—
Mother has sold her bed,
    Better to die than wed;
Where shall she lay her head?—
    Home she has none.
                    —*Ebenezer Elliott.*

THE UNIVERSAL DISTRESS

THE appalling living conditions of the poor was the immediate result of the general unemployment that prevailed in all parts of the country. The hand-loom weavers were the first victims of the depression of trade. As early as April 23, 1837, the *Manchester Times* recorded that " the distress has now reached the working classes. In this town and its neighborhood, many of the factories are working only four days a week, and some thousands of hand-loom weavers have been discharged ". The investigation made by the government showed that during the winter of 1837-1838 an almost unprecedented number of looms had been thrown into disuse not only in Manchester, but also in Spitalfields and other manufacturing centers.[1] Another commissioner reported that the applicants for relief were mostly able-bodied men with families, and widows with children, all of whom were driven to seek parish assistance

[1] *Report by Mr. Hickson on the Condition of the Hand-Loom Weavers, Presented to Parliament by Her Majesty's Command,* 1840, p. 4.

through lack of employment.[1] Dr. Kay's Report of 1837 on the distress of the Spitalfields weavers stated that out of the 14,000 looms, one-third were not used, while the remaining number were only partially employed. The manufacturers themselves estimated that the decrease in the work executed amounted to one-half the quantity ordinarily produced, and that the aggregate weekly wages of the weavers shrank from £10,000 or £12,000 to £5,000 or £6,000. The effect of this stagnation of trade can be realized when we bear in mind that even at their best, i. e. when employment was constant and regular, the weavers were, according to the report, so destitute of resources that the employers had to advance them money from week to week to defray the current expenses of their families.[2] The wages of the luckier weavers who retained their places were reduced from twenty-five to thirty per cent. The annual loss to the poor in nominal wages in Bolton alone was estimated in 1841 at £130,000.[3] The unoccupied houses in Preston numbered 1220, while in Oldham, out of the 7853 houses and shops, 1200 were empty as a result of total or partial unemployment.[4]

The industrial depression spread like a plague from town to town and from industry to industry, tightening its grip on England for more than half a decade. In Birmingham the labor aristocracy, the iron workers began to feel the

[1] *Report by Edward Gulson, respecting Nottingham, to Poor Law Commissioners*, 1837, p. 7.

[2] James Ph. Kay, *Report, Relative to the Distress Prevalent among the Spitalfields Weavers, to the Poor Law Commissioners*, London, 1837, pp. 1-2. On the want of employment of the hand-loom weavers in Scotland, see *Assistant Hand-loom Weavers' Commissioners' Report* of 1839, pp. 8-9.

[3] Hansard, *op. cit.*, vol. lviii, p. 31.

[4] *Ibid.*, pp. 593-594.

pinch of bad times in the early part of 1837. In March of that year a deputation submitted to Lord Melbourne a memorial, signed by " merchants, manufacturers and other inhabitants " of Birmingham, in which " the serious and immediate attention of His Majesty's Government " was solicited to the " general state of difficulty and embarrassment, threatening the most alarming consequences to all classes of the community ". The government was advised that " unless remedial measures be immediately applied, a large proportion of our population will shortly be thrown out of employment ".[1] The *laissez-faire* policy, however, was not abandoned, and no serious attempt was made to save the situation, with the result that by the end of 1842 there was hardly a single industry which was not in a critical state.[2] Archibald Prentice testifies that in 1841 there were 20,936 persons in Leeds, " whose average earnings were only elevenpence three-farthings a week. In Paisley, nearly one-fourth of the population was in a state bordering upon actual starvation. In one district, in Manchester, the Rev. Mr. Beardsall visited 258 families, consisting of 1029 individuals, whose average earnings were only sevenpence halfpenny per head per week."[3]

The agricultural districts could by no means boast of better conditions. The investigation of the state of three typical families of husbandmen in the union of Ampthill revealed that the means of living had been reduced, in money, from 1s. 8d. a head per week in 1834 to 1s. 2½d. in 1837, notwithstanding the fact that the work of these husbandmen had been increased from an aggregate of 39 weeks

---

[1] Bronterre's *National Reformer*, March 18, 1837.

[2] See Hansard, *op. cit.*, vol. lix, p. 636, and vol. lxiii, p. 1128.

[3] Archibald Prentice, *History of the Anti-Corn Law League*, London, 1853, vol. i, p. 270.

in 1834 to 142 in 1837. Moreover, this does not tell the whole story. The command that money had over bread in these two years must be taken into consideration. The average price of wheat in 1834 was 46s. 2d. per quarter, while in 1837 it reached 55s. 9d. The purchasing power of the earnings of the three families (which in 1834 and 1837 numbered 17 and 21 souls respectively) was 32 quarters of wheat, or 18½ pints per week for each person in 1834; whereas in 1837 their income could purchase only 23½ quarters of wheat, i. e., 11 pints per week for each person. In other words, the actual wages fell 41 per cent in comparison with the wages in 1834 which even then were far from adequate for a decent livelihood.[1] The investigation of the state of forty-eight families of husbandmen of the Ampthill union whose employment had been irregular, showed, that, notwithstanding the 760 weeks more work done in 1837 than in 1834, they suffered a reduction in their weekly money income per head of from 1s. 10½d. during 1834 to 1s. 6d. in 1837, or 20 per cent in nominal wages, and in the purchasing power of the latter expressed in wheat, a weekly reduction from 20¾ pints per head in 1834 to 13¾ pints per head in 1837, or a net reduction of 34 per cent.[2] The survey of thirty families of the same union, whose employment in husbandry had been regular during the years 1834-1837, revealed a similar result. The average weekly reduction in their actual wages, expressed in terms of wheat, fell from 23 1-10 pints to 17 3-10 pints per head, while the reduction of the income of *ten* of these families reached 32 per

---

[1] See *Twenty-third Report from the Select Committee on the Poor Law Amendment Act*, London, 1838, appendix B, pp. 34-35.

[2] See *Twenty-sixth and Twenty-seventh Reports from the Select Committee on the Poor Law Amendment Act*, London, 1838, appendix A, pp 44-45.

cent, and *one* family numbering seven persons had to subsist on only 1¾d., *i. e.*, 1 3-10 pints of wheat per day.[1]

The Whigs came into power pledged to reforms which they could hardly accomplish. The campaign for the Reform Bill of 1832 carried with it a promise for the repeal of the Corn Laws which had been condemned as fostering the monopoly of landowners. On his death-bed, Jeremy Bentham rejoiced that the Reform Bill would assure the triumph of free-trade. In spite of their pledges, however, and in spite of the many petitions in favor of the repeal of the Corn Laws, the reform Parliament and the reform ministers put up the "not-the-time" plea and energetically fought such repeal. Instead of ameliorating the condition of the poor, the government continued its *laissez-faire* policy, and allowed the misery of the working class to be exceedingly aggravated by the relentless rise of prices of wheat.

TABLE I

Year.	Price of Wheat per Quarter.
1836	39*s*. 5*d*.
1837	52*s*. 6*d*.
1838	55*s*. 3*d*.
1839	69*s*. 4*d*.
1840	68*s*. 6*d*.

The value of the imported wheat in 1836 was 0.1 per cent of the whole import of Great Britain, whereas in 1839 wheat was twenty per cent of the entire value of imports, reaching

[1] *Twenty-sixth and Twenty-seventh Reports, op. cit.*, appendix B, pp. 46-47. Concerning the condition of six laborers in other parishes of the same union, see *Twenty-eighth Report from the Select Committee on the Poor Law Amendment Act*, London, 1838, appendix, pp. 24-25. The subsequent Reports of the Committee endeavored to weaken the impression produced by the former Reports, and sophisticated methods were employed to discredit not only the conclusions but even the veracity of Mr. Turner, a former member of the Committee.

a sum never exceeded before (£10.5 million). This rise in the price of wheat taxed the working population of Bolton, for instance, as much as £195,000, which together with the reduction in wages amounted to a net loss of £325,000.[1] It goes without saying that this sudden rise in the price of wheat, due primarily to the high import duties, at the time of a well-nigh universal state of unemployment, robbed many families of the bare necessities of life. In one case a man was seen standing over a swill tub, into which was thrown the wash for the pigs, and taking several pieces out and eating them with a voracious appetite.[2] A farmer testified that about twenty females from Crompton and Shaw, near Oldham, begged him to allow them to disinter the body of a cow which had been buried a day and a half. Upon his permission the women " disinterred the body, cut it into pieces, took it to their respective families, who not only ate heartily of the carrion, but declared the meat to be the best they had tasted for many months past ".[3]

In Johnstone mothers were witnessed who divided a farthing salt herring and a half-pennyworth of potatoes among a family of seven; others mixed sawdust with oatmeal in making their porridge, to enable each to have a mouthful, while still other families lived for ten days on beans and peas and ears of wheat stolen from the neighboring fields.[4] Children wrangled with one another in the streets for the offal which well-to-do people did not allow their dogs to eat. Starving families seized the vilest substances which could protract for a few hours their miserable existence. Half-dressed wretches crowded together to save

---

[1] Hansard, *op. cit.*, vol. lviii, p. 31; vol. lxiii, p. 1125.

[2] *Ibid.*, vol. lviii, p. 595.

[3] *Ibid.* See also affidavit to the same effect in vol. lxiii, p. 26.

[4] *Ibid.*, vol. lix, p. 759.

themselves from the pain of cold. Several women were
found in the middle of the day imprisoned in one bed under
a blanket, because as many others who had on their backs
all the articles of dress that belonged to the party were out
of doors.[1]   Colonel T. P. Thompson, describing in the *Sun*
the distress he witnessed in Bolton in 1841, says:

I think I know what is the minimum of help by which horse,
ass, dog, hog or monkey can sustain existence, and where it
must go out for want of appliance and means of living.   But
anything like the squalid misery, the slow, moulding, putrifying death by which the weak and the feeble of the working
classes are perishing here, it never befel my eyes to behold,
nor my imagination to conceive.[2]

Such conditions being the rule and not the exception,
there is little wonder that various diseases took root in the
poor quarters and became the scourge of all industrial
cities.   Consumption and febrile diseases of a malignant and
fatal character, together with plagues, prevailed in almost
every house, and raised the mortality of the population to a
point threatening almost racial extermination.   The *Reports
of the Sanitary Condition of the Laboring Population of
England*, as well as the *Parliamentary Reports*, contain an
amazing mass of evidence to that effect.   In Liverpool, for
example, the average longevity of the gentry and profes-
sionals in 1840 was 35 years; that of business men and
skilled mechanics, 22 years, while that of day-laborers, operatives, *etc.*, was only 15 years.   The variation of mortality
in different districts of the metropolis in 1838 amounted.
according to the first annual report of the registrar-general,
to 100 per cent.   The report of one of the medical officers

[1] *Report on Sanitary Condition of the Laboring Population of Great
Britain*, 1842, p. 24.

[2] Quoted by Archibald Prentice, *op. cit.*, vol. i, p. 270.

stated explicitly that the dwelling condition in Liverpool was the source of many diseases, " particularly catarrh, rheumatic affections, and tedious cases of *typhus mitior*, which, owing to the overcrowded state of the apartment, occasionally pass into *typhus gravior* ". The cellars especially became hot-beds of epidemic diseases. In 1837 the same medical officer attended " a family of thirteen, twelve of whom had typhus fever, without a bed in the cellar, without straw or timber shavings—frequent substitutes. They lay on the floor, and so crowded, that I could scarcely pass between them ". In another house, fourteen patients were found lying on boards, and during their illness, had never removed their clothes.[1] Nassau W. Senior testified that he had found in Manchester a whole street following the course of a ditch, because in this way deeper cellars could be had without the cost of digging, and that not a single house of that street had escaped the cholera.[2] The extent of the spread of diseases in industrial centers can be realized from the fact that the total number of patients admitted to the dispensaries in the Manchester district during the six years ending in 1836 was 54,000, whereas the total number of those admitted during the six years of dear food ending in 1841 reached 169,000,—an increase of over 200 per cent.[3]

The opponents of the New Poor Law pointed out repeatedly that the new measure would propagate crime. Cobbett was particularly emphatic on this point. Robbery, murder and violence would become a matter of dire neces-

---

[1] See *Report on the Handloom Weavers*, 1841, vol. x, p. 350; *cf.* also *Report on the Sanitary Condition of the Laboring Population of Great Britain*, 1842, pp. 17-25.

[2] Nassau W. Senior, *Letters on the Factory Act to the Rt. Hon. the President of the Board of Trade*, London, 1837, p. 24.

[3] Hansard, *op. cit.*, vol. lxiii, p. 1124.

sity, prophesied he.[1] "What remains for the laborer but plunder?"—protested another.—"There is no law for a starving man—there is no tie of conscience or principle binding on a famished wretch who hears a wife and children clamorous for food."[2] The prophecies soon became facts. Offenses of the most heinous nature spread with epidemic rapidity over the whole country and especially in the manufacturing districts. The total expense for suppression of crime in 1841 amounted to the enormous sum of £604,165, the expense for a single convict being equal to the cost of education of one hundred and seventeen children. The loss by plunder at Liverpool alone amounted in that year to £700,000.[3] The progress of crime can be seen from the following table:[4]

TABLE II

Year	Population of England and Wales	% of Increase each year	Number of commitments	Proportion of commitments to population	% of Increase each years
1836	14,909,000	....	20,984	1 in 710	....
1837	15,105,000	1.3	23,612	1 in 639	12.5
1838	15,307,000	1.3	23,094	1 in 662	—2.1
1839	15,511,000	1.3	24,443	1 in 634	5.8
1840	15,718,000	1.3	27,187	1 in 578	11.2
1841	15,927,000	1.3	27,760	1 in 673	2.1
1842	16,141,000	1.3	31,309	1 in 516	12.8
Total increase during period	1,232,000	8.3	10,325	....	49.2

[1] Hansard, vol. xxiv, p. 1052.

[2] George Stephen, *Letter to the Rt. Hon. Lord John Russell on the Probable Increase of Rural Crime*, London, 1836, p. 4.

[3] Hansard, vol. lxvii, p. 66.

[4] See *Official Report of 1846*, no. 460, in vol. xxv. The increase of population as deduced from Census returns is even smaller. Thus, according to the Census reports, the total population in 1836 was 14,-758,000, and in 1842, 15,981,000—an increase of 12,000 less than in our table.

Of the commitments of 1842 not less than 8,591, or nearly 28 per cent, were made in the two manufacturing districts of Lancashire and Middlesex, including London, although the population of those districts was far from constituting such a large percentage of the total. The official report of Lancashire showed that the increase of crime in that district was nearly six times as great as that of the population.

The Poor Law Commissioners could boast of the effect of their measures which brought about an annual average saving of a couple of millions in the expenditures for poor relief. But England paid too high a price for these sterling pounds by forcing multitudes of people into the " bastiles ". The wretchedness of the situation can be gauged from the growing number of workhouse inmates as shown in the following table. Bearing in mind that nothing but actual starvation could force the people to entetr the relief-prisons, such an increase tells a sorry tale. Within five years the workhouse population of England and Wales almost doubled.

TABLE III[1]

Year	Persons in receipt of outdoor relief	Cumulative Increase during the period	Cumulative per cent of increase	Persons in workhouses	Cumulative Increase during the period	Cumulative per cent of increase	Difference in the per cent of increase
1839....	997,000	....	....	140,000	....	....	....
1840....	1,030,000	33,000	3.3	169,000	29,000	20.7	17.4
1841....	1,108,000	111,000	11.0	192,000	52,000	37.0	26.0
1842....	1,196,000	199,000	20.0	223,000	83,000	59.3	39.3
1843....	1,300,000	303,000	30.3	239,000	99,000	70.7	40.4

Table III shows clearly that while the stringent administrators of the New Poor Law began to discern the hand-

[1] This table is constructed on the basis of data given in Hansard, op. cit., vol. lxv, p. 367, vol. lxvi, pp. 1178-1179, and in George Nichols' History of the English Poor Law, London, 1854, vol. ii, p. 375.

writing on the wall and granted out-door relief to a greater number of applicants than immediately after the introduction of the new measure, their ideal means of succor was still the workhouse. And all this in face of the universal indignation which was manifested throughout the whole country. There is no wonder, then, that Tory politicians, as well as radical friends of labor, were remorseless in their denunciation of both the Whigs and their New Poor Law. The hatred displayed by the Tories was nurtured by their instinctive fear of the newly-formed capitalist class which began to assert its power in quite an arrogant way. But it was this very acquisition of power by the middle class that caused the apprehension of the radicals. Their name was legion who believed with Bronterre, even as early as 1837, that the object of the New Poor Law was to reduce labor " to the lowest rate of remuneration at which existence can be sustained ". The new class was pictured as a band of " the greatest tyrants over the people ", since " the most formidable, as well as the most remorseless of all despotisms, is the despotism of money ".[1]

The last session of Parliament in 1838 was bombarded with petitions bearing the signatures of 269,000 persons who requested the repeal of the new measure, whereas only thirty-five petitions with 952 signatures were presented in favor of retention of the New Poor Law. The people felt themselves outraged and expressed their resentment at public meetings, some of which were attended by crowds whose numbers were estimated at 300,000.[2] The Whigs, however, were not to be daunted, and the party in power continued to remain brutally heedless to the desperate cry of millions of men and women.

[1] See Bronterre's *National Reformer*, January 28, Feb. 11 and March 18, 1837.

[2] Hansard, *op. cit.*, vol. xli, 1838, pp. 1005-1006.

CHAPTER V

> Call Chartism by what name you
> will, its principles have sprung from
> the infant blood of English children;
> and though you water them with the
> blood of millions, yet, by the God who
> made us all equal, I swear that I will
> take the little children, their fathers,
> and their mothers, out of your toils
> and grasp, or die in the attempt!
> —*Feargus O'Connor.*

LABOR LEGISLATION AND TRADE UNIONISM

THE working class was keenly disappointed in the
Whigs for their hostile attitude towards labor legislation.
It was the ultra Tories, Richard Oastler, Michael Thomas
Sadler and Lord Ashley [1] who led the campaign against the

---

[1] Richard Oastler (1789-1861), the "king of the factory children,"
was a Tory and an advocate of the abolition of slavery in the West
Indies. He led the agitation for the ten-hour day from 1830 on-
wards. In 1830 he began his series of fiery letters to the *Leeds Mercury*, and afterwards to the *Leeds Intelligencer*, on the "Yorkshire
Slavery." He vigorously opposed the New Poor Law, and was imprisoned for debt in 1840; the Whigs repeatedly offered to pay his
debt and confer other favors upon him if he would give up his agitation against the Poor Laws. He refused to make any deal with his
conscience, and for three years remained in prison, whence he published his *Fleet Papers*, in which he incessantly urged the need of factory reform and the abolition of the Poor Laws.

Michael Thomas Sadler (1780-1835), Tory, philanthropist and writer
on political economy, introduced a bill for restricting child labor in
1831. He was chairman of the Select Committee appointed to inquire
into the condition of the children employed in factories, and his solic-

evils of the factory system and demanded the amelioration
of workmen's conditions. The Short Time Committee was
justly described as a curious " combination of Socialists,
Chartists and ultra Tories ",[1] but the Whig representatives
were at all times conspicuous by their absence from among
those who fought the people's battle.[2]

The fight was forced on the advocates of labor legislation by the condition of the men, women and children who
were employed in factories. It started at the time when
the employers' demand for freedom of contract was in complete harmony with the *laissez-faire* doctrine of the economists. This doctrine proclaimed it a " natural law " that
employers and employees should be allowed to make what
arrangements they pleased between themselves, without interference on the part of the government. It required a
kind of philosophical courage, besides a warm feeling for
the exploited, to oppose the then prevailing notions of
social justice. When the Ten-Hour Movement grew
stronger, the ethical and abstract ideas were left to take
care of themselves, and the opponents of the movement
began to promulgate the economic or commercial argument
for which Nassau Senior stood sponsor. The whole ques-

itous and unremitting work was said to have been a contributing cause
to his premature death.

Anthony Ashley Cooper, Lord Ashley, afterwards Lord Shaftesbury
(1801-1885), Tory, became interested in factory children in 1832 and
introduced a Ten-Hour Bill in 1833. He was the most zealous advocate of labor legislation and an ardent social reformer.

[1] *The Leeds Mercury*, March 23, 1844.

[2] The most prominent leaders in the agitation against child labor, besides Oastler, Sadler and Ashley, were the Rev. J. R. Stephens, the
Chartist leader; John Doherty, the general secretary of the Federation
of Cotton Spinners, a Chartist; George Condy, the editor of the *Manchester and Salford Advertiser;* Philip Grant; and later the radical
John Fielden, who took Lord Ashley's place during his temporary re-
tirement from the House in 1846.

tion was then presented from the point of view of economic expediency. Starting with the assumption that in the cotton manufacture " the whole profit is derived from *the last hour* ", and that " if the hours of working were reduced by one hour per day, net profit would be destroyed; if they were reduced by an hour and a half, even gross profit would be destroyed ",—Senior reached the ingenious conclusion that it was in the interest of the working classes themselves to oppose the reduction of the hours of labor, which would be " attended by the most fatal consequences ". As to the exertion and overwork, Senior thought that the work of children and young persons in the cotton mills was " mere confinement, attention and attendance ", and it was scarcely possible to feel fatigue after " extremely long hours " of work.[1]

This last view of Mr. Senior was, to say the least, a preposterous denial of actual conditions. The government reports, as well as the accounts in contemporary newspapers and magazines, tell quite a different story. Dr. Kay, himself an opponent of state interference with the hours of labor, depicts the condition of the factory laborer in the following lines: " Whilst the engine runs the people must work,—men, women and children are yoked together with iron and steam. The animal machine—breakable in the best case, subject to a thousand sources of suffering,—is chained fast to the iron machine, which knows no suffering and no weariness." [2] Another opponent of the factory act, Mr. Roebuck, wrote from Glasgow in 1838 that he visited a cotton mill where he saw a sight that froze his blood.

[1] Nassau William Senior, *Letters on the Factory Act*, London, 1837, pp. 12-13.

[2] James Philip Kay, *Moral and Physical Conditions of the Operatives Employed in the Cotton Manufacture in Manchester*, 1832, p. 24.

The place was full of women, young all of them, some large with child, and obliged to stand twelve hours each day. Their hours are from five in the morning to seven in the evening, two hours of that being for rest, so that they stand twelve clear hours. The heat was excessive in some of the rooms, the stink pestiferous, and in all an atmosphere of cotton flue. I nearly fainted.[1]

The employment of women and children was attacked by Ashley and his followers on the ground that it inevitably breaks up the family. Of the 419,560 factory operatives in Great Britain in 1839, for instance, 192,887, or 46 per cent were under eighteen years of age; the 242,296 females included 112,192 girls under eighteen years of age. Only 96,569, or 23 per cent, were adult male operatives.[2] Women were reported to return to the factory three or four days after confinement and dripping wet with milk while at work.

The pestilent atmosphere and the inevitable contact of many people in one work-room had a detrimental effect on the morals of the factory employees. In Manchester three-fourths of such employees at the age of from fourteen to twenty years were reported unchaste.[3]

An estimate of sexual morality,—writes one of the commissioners,—cannot readily be reduced to figures; but if I may trust my own observations and the general opinion of those with whom I have spoken, as well as the whole tenor of the testimony furnished me, the aspect of the influence of factory life upon the morality of the youthful female population is most depressing.[4]

[1] R. E. Leader, *Life of Roebuck*, quoted by B. L. Hutchins and A. Harrison in the *History of Factory Legislation*, Westminster, 1903, pp. 91-92.

[2] See Ashley's Speech of March 15, 1844, in Hansard, *op. cit.*, vol. lxxiii.

[3] Cf. *Report from Commissioners Appointed to Collect Information in the Manufacturing Districts*, 1834, *Cowell Evidence*, p. 57.

[4] *Ibid., Hawkins' Report*, p. 4.

The report of the Select Committee also brought to light many facts in regard to the employment of children in factories. Children of five years of age were very few, but there was a considerable number of six-year-old and a still greater number of seven-year-old children; the greatest number, however, consisted of children of from eight to nine years of age. The working-day frequently lasted from fourteen to sixteen hours, and the children were under a cruel discipline of overseers who enforced authority by corporal punishment. The extremely long hours of work brought with them, Mr. Senior's assertion to the contrary notwithstanding, most serious consequences not only from the point of view of morality, but also from a purely physiological standpoint.[1] The commissioners' report contains abundant evidence of the horrible effect of the factory system on the population. Children were deformed, often seized naked in bed by overseers and driven with blows to the factory; women were made unfit for child-bearing; men were crippled; whole generations afflicted with disease. It was these monstrosities that roused the friends of the people to exclaim against the factory system. The discontent of the laborers, crude and sporadic in the beginning of the Industrial Revolution, assumed all the aspects of social war which stratified the population of Great Britain with marvelous rapidity. Criminal offenses against property were superseded by strikes, abortive and irresponsible in the beginning, but becoming ever more organized and systematic, as the divorce between the functions and interests of the employer and those of the workman became more inevitable with each stride of the capitalist régime.

[1] *Cf. ibid., Dr. Loudon Evidence,* pp. 12, 13 and 16; *Drinkwater Evidence,* pp. 72, 80, 146, 150 and 155; *Power Evidence,* pp. 63 and 66-69; *Sir D. Barry Evidence,* pp. 6, 8, 13, 21, 44 and 55; *Tufnell Evidence,* pp. 5, 6 and 16.

Attempts at trade unionism were made even in the beginning of the new factory system. Adam Smith had already observed that "people of the same trade seldom meet together, even for merriment and diversion, but the conversation ends in conspiracy against the public or in some contrivance to raise prices ".[1] There certainly were such "conspiracies" among the members of the working class. As early as 1806 the government reported the existence of some kind of a national union of clothworkers with a central committee at the head.[2] Benefit clubs and other associations were formed at the end of the eighteenth and the beginning of the nineteenth centuries both for the purpose of carrying on parliamentary agitation against the factory owners and for industrial combination and class struggle. Parliament, of course, was persistent in its *laissez-faire* policy and, in spite of the persevering demands of the operatives for a minimum rate of wages and a legal limitation of the number of apprentices, the House of Commons was more than once carried in the interests of members whose factories swarmed with children. Industrial combinations of workmen being legally forbidden and severely prosecuted during the first quarter of the nineteenth century, artisans were forced into a system of conspiracy against employers and of cruel treatment of non-unionists. The attempt of the workingmen at organized political agitation against the Combination Laws was immediately crushed by the notorious "Six Acts" of 1819. These laws suppressed well-nigh all public meetings, imposed a very high stamp duty on all labor publications and stringently enforced the law on seditious libels, thus exposing authors or publishers to the penalty of banishment from all

---

[1] *Wealth of Nations* (McCulloch's edition, 1863), book i, chap. x, p. 59.
[2] See *Report of the Committee on the Woollen Manufacture*, 1806, p. 16.

parts of his Majesty's dominion or of transportation to special places, if anything was printed which was not to the taste of the government.   There was, on the part of the latter, an evident determination to resort to nothing but force.   "They think of nothing else"—protested a member of Parliament,—"they dream of nothing else; they will try no means of conciliation; they will make no attempt to pacify and reconcile; force—force— force—and nothing but force".[1]   Radicalism was repre- sented as a spirit, "of which the first elements are a rejec- tion of Scripture, and a contempt of all the institutions of your country, and of which the results, unless averted by a merciful Providence, must be anarchy, atheism, and uni- versal ruin".[2]   Radicals were accordingly branded and treated as traitors.   "Orator" Hunt and Cobbett, the her- alds of the English labor movement, were abused, mal- treated, and, therefore, driven to extremes.   Even Francis Place,[3] the champion political wire-puller and labor lobby-

[1] Tierney in the House of Commons, as quoted in Walpole's *History of England*, vol. i, pp. 516-517.

[2] Walpole's *History of England*, vol. i, p. 426.

[3] Francis Place (1771-1854), a master tailor, was the son of a brutal father, who, to amuse himself, used to knock his children down.   In 1808 Place became acquainted with James Mill and Bentham, and soon became their pupil, associate, and friend; with Bentham, he was on affectionate terms.   In their letters they used to address one another, "My dear old father," and "Dear good boy," respectively.   Since 1818 he devoted all his time and energy to the agitation for the repeal of the Combination Laws and to the Reform movement, and proved himself a remarkable politician.   His shop at Charing Cross was the center of the radicals and reformers, and his "Civic Library" was a kind of rendezvous for members of Parliament and social agitators of all sorts.   He was to a great extent responsible for the diffusion of the Benthamite ideas among the English-speaking people.   His rôle in the repeal of the Combination Laws was that of an organizer and political wire-puller.   He was a great collector of social, economic and labor facts, and his invaluable manuscript records are now in the possession of the British Museum.   A not inconsiderable portion of the economic tracts collected and annotated by him is in the library of Professor Edwin R. A. Seligman.

ist, for a long time could hardly secure a hearing in Parliament. But his victory in 1825, securing to the working class the right of collective bargaining, proved mere sectional combination ineffective as long as the government machinery remained in the hands of the employers. Then came the reform of 1832 which substituted one set of political masters for another, and dampened the enthusiasm of the working class for political reforms. For a time the stratagem of the labor leaders was conducted on an exclusively industrial plan and the social war acquired a still more formidable aspect. Trade unionism became the battle-cry of the friends of the laborers, and the employers were thrown into a state of extreme apprehension. New hopes were infused into the hearts of the lowly, and a new creed was given them by Robert Owen and his followers. Paliative remedies in the form of social legislation began to be despised. There was a bigger thing for the working class to do—to reconstruct the whole society on a new basis.

The practical Utopia of Owen was backed by the theoretical doctrines of the then popular socialist writers. Charles Hall's admirable work *The Effects of Civilization on the People in European States* preached a social crusade, while William Godwin's *Political Justice* pointed to the system of private property as the root of all social evil. The writings of William Thompson, Thomas Hodgskin, John Gray, and the minor so-called Ricardian socialists, taught the propertyless that labor was the only universal measure and characteristic distinction of wealth and that labor should, therefore, enjoy the whole produce of its exertions, while, on the other hand, every individual who did not apply *his own hands* to the factors of production,—all merchants, manufacturers, clerks, shopmen, directors, superintendents,—was a direct tax upon the manual laborer.[1] All these doctrines strongly tended to promote the formation of Owenite societies.

A characteristic description of the Owenite intoxication of that period is given by Francis Place:

The nonsensical doctrine preached by Robert Owen and others respecting communities and goods in common; abundance of everything man ought to desire, and all for four hours' labor out of every twenty-four; the right of every man to his share of the earth in common, and his right to whatever his hands had been employed upon; the power of masters under the present system to give just what wages they pleased; the right of the laborer to such wages as would maintain him and his comfort for eight or ten hours' labor; the right of every man who was unemployed to employment and to such an amount of wages as has been indicated — and other matters of a similar kind which were continually inculcated by the workingmen's political unions, by many small knots of persons, printed in small pamphlets and handbills which were sold twelve for a penny and distributed to a great extent—had pushed politics aside, . . . among the working people. These pamphlets were written almost wholly by men of talent and of some standing in the world, professional men, gentlemen, manufacturers, tradesmen, and men called literary. The consequences were that a very large proportion of the working people in England and Scotland became persuaded that they had only to combine, as it was concluded they might easily do, to compel not only a considerable advance of wages all round, but employment for every one, man and woman, who needed it, at short hours. This notion induced them to form themselves into Trades Unions in a manner and to an extent never before known.[2]

The wage-earner, however, soon experienced a bitter dis-

[1] See Professor Edwin R. A. Seligman, "On Some Neglected British Economists," in the *Economic Journal*, vol. xiii, 1903.

[2] See Sidney and Beatrice Webb, *History of Trade Unionism*, 1902, pp. 141-142.

appointment which he felt the more because of his high aspirations.   Taught by the gospel of Utopia to despise specific, regulative and immediate remedies, and to strive for one which would apply to all social evils and to all iniquities, he acquired an aggressive and haughty attitude towards the " unproductive " classes, provoking reciprocal hatred and stringent opposition from the latter.   The capitalists were naturally not loth to remove the " Day of Judgment " to as remote a future as they possibly could, and they saw to it that the new industrial organization, the " New Moral World ", should not " come suddenly upon society like a thief in the night ".   In fact, their watch was so alert that the strongest trades unions came to grief as soon as they attempted to realize their humblest plans.   The aggressive policy of the laborers encountered a still more determined opposition not only on the part of the employers but also of the government.   In this case the latter enjoyed the fruit of the wisdom of Nassau Senior, who, as commissioner appointed to inquire into the state of combinations and strikes, recorded his conviction, which was based exclusively on statements and hearsay gossip of employers, that " the general evils and general dangers of combinations cannot easily be exaggerated ", that " if a few agitators can command and enforce a strike which first paralyzes the industry of the peculiar class of workpeople over whom they tyrannize, and then extends itself in an increasing circle over the many thousands and tens of thousands to whose labor the assistance of that peculiar class of workpeople is essential . . . that if this state of things is to continue, we shall not retain the industry, the skill, or the capital, on which our manufacturing superiority, and, with that superiority, our power and almost our existence as a nation, depends ".[1]

[1] Nassau W. Senior, *Historical and Philosophical Essays*, London, 1865, vol. ii, p. 171.

The employers stopped short of nothing until they had succeeded in defeating and crushing the labor organizations. Even the most popular *Grand National Consolidated Trades Union* which was started, through the agitation of Robert Owen, in 1834, and which enrolled within a few weeks at least half a million members, men and women of various trades, was exterminated by the combination of employers who resorted to lock-outs in order to force the laborers to abandon the union. The conviction of many strikers and the barbarous sentences brought against them by the courts were enough to chill the most ardent followers of the new order.[1] Notice was served that a bill would be introduced to make combinations of trades impossible. Many a trades unionist began to suspect that the new moral world could not be ushered in without a hard struggle in the teeth of a hostile government, subservient commissioners and corrupt courts. Conspiracies, intimidation and violence on the part of workingmen began to show signs of something more dangerous than the talk of some future Day of Judgment. The capitalists, however, blinded by their easy victories, were unable to read the handwriting on the wall. Union after union was disbanded and crushed by the newly-formed Chamber of Commerce, thus driving multitudes of people into the very pit of revolution. " Back to politics!" became the slogan of the bulk of laborers. Politics again became the emblem of something which could give everything and deprive of everything; Parliament began to be regarded with awe as a new Almighty in whose word lay life and death. And it was quite natural. The workingmen lost their battle on the industrial field, and they lost it because the machinery of government was turned against them. The important point of stratagem appeared to lie in the

[1] See George Loveless, *The Victims of Whiggery*, London, 1837.

capture of that machinery and its use against the capitalists. The New Poor Law, the hostility and treachery of the government and the crushing defeat of labor organizations brought, to use Cobbett's words on an earlier occasion, the issue of the working class " to be a question of actual starvation or fighting for food; and when it comes to that point, I know that Englishmen will never lie down and die by hundreds by the wayside." [1]

The apotheosis of political power brought again the issue of universal suffrage to the foreground. The foremost radical writers renewed their fight for " freedom ". Bronterre started his *National Reformer* on the 7th of January, 1837, with the declaration that the " money monster " must be fought with his own weapons:

Government, Law, Property, Religion, and *Morals*, these five words embrace everything that affects our happiness as social beings, and consequently all that a reformer can have to deal with. I place *Government* at the head, because upon *that* do all the rest really depend. It is the *Government* that makes the law. The *law* determines the property—and on the *state of property* depend the *religion* and *morals*, and (as a consequence) the *well-being* and *happiness* of every people in the world. . . . The parent cause (of the wretched condition of the people) being bad government, we must necessarily begin with that—and if the government be bad, because, as I contend, it is wrongly constituted, *our first attempt must be to have it constituted rightly*. Here, then, I am at once conducted to my old ground, *universal suffrage*. A government which does not represent the interests of all who are called upon to obey its laws, is necessarily a wrongly constituted government.

In his article on " Social Occupations " in the same issue

---

[1] See the *Political Register*, October 20, 1815.

he dwells at some length on the same question and upbraids the masses for their want of sufficient interest in universal suffrage. Says he:

I know but one way of salvation for us—but one way of felling the *monster* without being buried underneath his ruins; *it is to smite him with the authority of the law, having first got the law on the people's side.* It is only by having first got the law on *his* side, that he has been able to prostrate us. Why should not we be able to do the same by him when we have got the law on ours? . . . What right has he to exclude you more than you to exclude him? . . . I am, therefore, obliged, —reluctantly, but unavoidably obliged—to conclude that your exclusion is the work of your own ignorant and craven submission. You have made no bold efforts as a body—no grand· demonstrations to obtain the franchise; you have occasionally petitioned, it is true, but your petitions were " few and far between ", they were also weak and desultory, seldom bold and commanding — never simultaneous and absorbing. You talked in them about your paying taxes, and being liable to serve in the militia, and all that sort of unconsequential rubbish, but you never put forward your claims resolutely, as men who had an equal, and even a superior stake in the question, to that of your oppressors—namely, your very lives, which are hourly threatened with destruction by the murderous *money-monster*. Much less did you meet simultaneously, and in millions, to demonstrate the absorbing interest you took in the question. On the contrary, you were satisfied, even in your best days, to abandon your case to the care of a few demagogues, who, however honest and brave, could do nothing for you without some grand national movement on your own part.

The reproach of Bronterre came at a time when the seeds of discontent had already begun to sprout to the surface. The " grand national movement " was on its way. It was but a short time after those lines had been penned that from the ruins of trade unionism arose a magnificent tower which, for over a decade, allured the misery-stricken lowly, and illumined the way for millions of devoted and heroic men and women.

The name of that tower was Chartism.

CHAPTER VI

Knaves will tell you that it is because you have no property you are
unrepresented. I tell you, on the contrary, it is because you are unrepresented that you have no property.
—*Bronterre.*

THE PEOPLE'S CHARTER

THE London Working Men's Association was organized
on the 16th of June, 1836, under the leadership of men who
for a number of years had been associated with various
phases of the labor movement. Henry Hetherington and
John Cleave, the champions of a free unstamped press, William Lovett, Henry Vincent, George Julian Harney and
other prominent members of trade unions, little thought then
that the movement which they inaugurated was destined to
play such a revolutionary rôle in the life of the English
working class. Humble, indeed, were the objects which
the association set for itself to achieve. Liberalism, Radicalism, Trade Unionism, Socialism, Owenism and Rotund-
ism, were reduced to the following lowest common denomin-
ators:[1]

1. To draw into one bond of *unity* the *intelligent* and *influential* portion of the working classes in town and country.

2. To seek by every legal means to place all classes of society
in possession of their equal political and social rights.

3. To devise every possible means, and to use every exertion,
to remove those cruel laws that prevent the free circulation of
thought through the medium of a *cheap and honest press.*

[1] See *Address and Rules of the Working Men's Association, for
Benefiting Socially and Morally the Useful Classes,* London, 1836.

4. To promote, by all available means, the education of the rising generation, and the extirpation of those systems which tend to future slavery.

5. To collect every kind of information appertaining to the interests of the working classes in particular and society in general, especially statistics regarding the wages of labor, the habits and condition of the laborer, and all those that mainly contribute to the present state of things.

6. To meet and communicate with each other for the purpose of digesting the information required, and to mature such plans as they believe will conduce in practice to the well-being of the working classes.

7. To publish their views and sentiments in such form and manner as shall best serve to create a moral, reflecting, yet energetic public opinion; so as eventually to lead to a gradual improvement in the condition of the working classes, *without violence or commotion.*

8. To form a library of reference and useful information; to maintain a place where they can associate for mental improvement, and where their brethren from the country can meet with kindred minds actuated by one great motive—that of benefiting politically, socially, and morally, the useful classes.

In this address, calling upon the working class to form similar societies, the association cautions " strictly to adhere to a judicious selection of their members." The working-men are exhorted to make " the principles of democracy as respectable in practice as they are just in theory, by excluding the drunken and immoral from our ranks and uniting in close compact with the honest, sober, moral and thinking portion of our brethren."

The rules of the association made only workingmen eligible for membership. The card issued by the association to its members contained the following maxim: " The man who evades his share of useful labor diminishes the public stock of wealth and throws his own burden upon

his neighbor." Persons not of the " industrious classes "
were admitted only as honorary members and could participate in the debates and discussions and attend all meetings, but were debarred from holding any office or from
taking any part in the management of the organization.

The exclusiveness of the association was the direct result of former experiences with radical representatives of
the middle class. Lovett tells only half of the story
when he attributes the fixed rule of exclusiveness to a desire
" to try an experiment," in order to evince the discrimina-
tion and independent spirit in the management of their political affairs, in which the workingmen were found wanting.
" The masses and their political organizations were taught
to look up to *great men* (or to men *professing greatness*)
rather than to great principles. We wished, therefore, to establish a political school of self-instruction among them,
in which they should accustom themselves to examine great
social and political principles." [1]

The address published by the association, however, be-
trays the real cause:

It has been said by some that our objects are exclusive, seeing
we wish to confine our association to workingmen. We reply,
that judging from experience and appearance, the political
and social regeneration of the working classes must be begun
by themselves, and, therefore, they should not admit any preponderating influence of wealth or title to swerve them from
their duty. . . . Let not, however, the men of wealth imagine
that we have any ulterior designs inimical to their rights, or
views opposed to the peace and harmony of society. On the
contrary, we seek to render property more secure; life more
sacred; and to preserve inviolate every institution that can be
made to contribute to the happiness of man. We only seek

[1] William Lovett, *Life and Struggles*, pp. 91-92.

that share in the institutions and government of our country
which our industry and usefulness justly merit.

The address was signed by Henry Hetherington, treasurer, and William Lovett, secretary, but was apparently composed by men of various creeds. It expressed no clear-cut
principle; it held forth no fixed ideal. While it consoled the
men of wealth with the assertion that the association had
no ulterior or sinister designs, that it did not intend " to get
a transfer of wealth, power or influence for a party," it also
vowed to probe social evils to their source and " to apply
effective remedies to prevent instead of unjust laws to punish." The source of social evils, not clearly visible in this
declaration, was revealed, however, in a subsequent address
of the association to the working classes of Belgium, issued
in November, 1836. Starting with the interesting assertion
that "the cause of those foolish dissentions between nations
lies in the *ignorance* " of the workingmen of their position
in society, the address continues :

Ignorance has caused us to believe that *we* were " born to
toil," and *others* to enjoy—that we were naturally *inferior*, and
should silently bow to the government of those who were
pleased to call themselves *superior*; and consequently those
who have governed us have done so for their own advantage,
and not ours. . . . Their laws have been enacted to perpetuate their power, and administered to generate fear and submission towards self-constituted greatness, hereditary ignorance, or wealth, however unjustly acquired. . . . Our emancipation, however, will depend on the extent of this knowledge among the working classes of all countries, or its salutary
effects in causing us to perceive *our real position in society*—
in causing us to feel that we, being the producers of wealth,
have the *first claim* to its enjoyment.[1]

[1] William Lovett, *op. cit.*, p. 98.

The association recognized the importance of political power from the beginning and set forth its views in a three-penny pamphlet—*The Rotten House of Commons*.[1] The pamphlet contained statistical information on the composition of Parliament.   The tables were compiled from Parliamentary returns and from the elaborate works of reputable statisticians.   They showed that $\frac{1}{147}$ of the entire population, or $\frac{1}{30}$ of the adult males above the age of twenty-one, had the power of passing all the laws in the House of Commons, which would be binding upon all inhabitants of England.   The proportion of registered electors who had the vote to the number of males above twenty-one years of age in the United Kingdom was about 1 to 7½.   The composition of the reformed House of Commons was shown to consist exclusively of members of the nobility, of the army and navy, the barristers and solicitors and of the moneyed classes.

The people of England were invited to reflect on the question whether the working classes had fit representatives in the great number of land-holders, money-makers, speculators, usurers, lords, earls, and other honorables, as well as in the number of military and navy representatives, barristers, solicitors, *etc.*

Are the *manufacturer* and *capitalist*, whose exclusive monopoly of the combined powers of wood, iron, and steam, enables them to cause the destitution of thousands, and who have an interest in forcing labor down to the *minimum* reward, fit to represent the interests of working men?   Is the *master*, whose interest it is to purchase labor at the cheapest rate, a fit representative for the *workman*, whose interest it is to get the most he can for his labor?

[1] *The Rotten House of Commons, being an Exposition of the Present State of the Franchise, and an Appeal to the Nation of the Course to be Pursued in the Approaching Crisis*, Hetherington, Strand.

The association urged the laborers to refuse to be the tools of any party who will not, as a *first and essential measure*, give to the working classes *equal political and social rights*, so that they may send their own representatives, from the ranks of those who live by labor,

to deliberate and determine along with *all other interests*, that the interests of the laboring classes—of those who are the foundation of the social edifice—shall not be daily sacrificed to glut the extravagance of the pampered few.   If you feel with us, then you will proclaim it in the workshop, preach it in your societies, publish it from town to village, from county to county, and from nation to nation, that there is no hope for the sons of toil, till those who feel with them, who sympathise with them, and whose interests are identified with theirs, *have an equal right to determine what laws shall be enacted or plans adopted* for justly governing this country.

The association had Hetherington's weekly " Twopenny Despatch " at its disposal.   It was not satisfied, however, with printed propaganda alone.   Immediately upon its formation, Hetherington, Vincent and Cleave were engaged to make an agitation tour all over the country.   They depicted the wrongs of the toiling classes and fanned the passions of the people into a flame.   Within a very short time they were successful in organizing a great number of workingmen's associations.   Encouraged by the general response of the masses, the association published a petition for a new Parliamentary Constitution.   The petition contained the essence of the pamphlet—*The Rotten House of Commons*, and was commented upon by the radical writers as one of the most important documents.   Brontèrre reprinted it in his *National Reformer* of February 11, 1837, with the following editorial remarks " to the unrepresented millions ":

I have seen few documents that comprise so many important

facts within an equal space; I have not seen any which reflects the *mind* of indignant industry with brighter effect; or which, as a clear and powerful exposition of the wrongs inflicted on you, and of the rights withheld, is better calculated to challenge regard and sympathy in your behalf.

The petition was drawn up by William Lovett and contained the nucleus of the subsequently famous People's Charter.[1]   The House of Commons was requested to enact a law with the following " six points ":

(1) Equal Representation.
(2) Universal Suffrage.
(3) Annual Parliaments.
(4) No Property Qualifications.
(5) Vote by Ballot.
(6) Payments to Members.

On the 28 of February, 1837, a great public meeting was held in London, at the Crown and Anchor, under the auspices of the London Working Men's Association, at which, after the petition was approved and signed by about three thousand persons, a unanimous resolution was carried to present it to Parliament.   Having no representatives of their own, the association entrusted the petition to J. A. Roebuck, who was at that time considered the most staunch advocate of democratic principles in the House of Commons. On his advice, the association issued a circular to all radical members of Parliament to meet at the British Coffee-house, in Cockspur Street, on the 3rd of May, 1837, and at this meeting, which was attended by several members of the House, including Daniel O'Connell, Joseph Hume, Colonel T. P. Thompson, W. S. Crawford, J. T. Leader and others, Lovett introduced the subject on the part of the association.

[1] See Appendix A.

The discussions which lasted for two evenings resulted in the unanimous adoption of four important resolutions. In the first, the members of Parliament agreed to support Representative Roebuck in his proposition for universal suffrage. In the second, they pledged themselves to support and vote for any bill embodying " the principles of universal suffrage, equal representation, free selection of representatives without reference to property, the ballot, and short parliaments of fixed duration, the limit not to exceed three years." The third resolution bound them to support and vote for a bill for such reform of the House of Lords as shall render it responsible to the people. The fourth resolution provided that a committee of twelve be appointed to draw up a bill in a legal form embodying the above principles and to submit it to another joint meeting. These resolutions were signed by Daniel O'Connell, Charles Hindley, W. S. Crawford, J. T. Leader, John Fielden, T. Wakley, D. W. Harvey, T. P. Thompson, J. A. Roebuck, and Dr. Bowring. The committee appointed to draw up the bill consisted of O'Connell, Roebuck, Leader, Hindley, Colonel Thompson, Crawford, Lovett, Hetherington, Vincent, Cleave, J. Watson, and R. Moore,—the last six being members of the association.

The death of William IV led to the prorogation of Parliament. On this occasion, the association issued an address to reformers on the forthcoming elections, urging that only those candidates should be returned, who would pledge themselves to universal suffrage and " all the other essentials of self-government." It was in this address that the association for the *first time* referred to the " six points " as the *People's Charter*.

The address was circulated among all workingmen's associations and political unions. It was at this juncture that the famous Birmingham Political Union which had kept

aloof from the new political agitation declared itself in favor
of the petition.   The Birmingham laborers were considered
the aristocracy of the working class; the political union enjoyed the reputation of having been greatly responsible for
the successful issue of the campaign for the Reform Bill
of 1832.   The entrance of the Birmingham union into a
new campaign for universal suffrage was, therefore, hailed
by the workingmen's associations as a singular victory for
their cause.   Their satisfaction was particularly enhanced
after the publication by the union of an address, in which
it confessed its disappointment with the Whigs and attributed the distress of the people to the discredited Reform
Bill:

The motive and end of all legislation is the happiness of the
universal people.   Let us try the Reform Bill by that test.
. . . What do we find?   Merchants bankrupt, workmen unemployed and starving, workhouses crowded, factories deserted, distress and dissatisfaction everywhere prevalent. . . .
Were the people fully and fairly represented in Parliament,
would such things be?

.

    After the accession of Queen Victoria, the London
Working Men's Association in conjunction with other organizations prepared an address to Her Majesty.   An exchange of correspondence took place between Lovett and
Lord John Russell, then Secretary of State for the Home
Department.   Lovett requested that a deputation of six persons be presented personally to the Queen.   Russell replied
that the deputation would have to wait until Her Majesty
held a levee, and that they must attend in court dress.
Lovett's retort was that they had "neither the means nor
the inclination to indulge in such absurdities as dress coats
and wigs", and he expressed the hope that the day was not
distant, when some better means would be devised " for

letting the sovereign hear of the addresses and petitions of the people." The address to the Queen, as well as the correspondence between Lovett and Russell, caused much comment in the press. In the address the Queen was asked to cause a bill to be introduced for the extension of the right of suffrage to all the adult population of the kingdom. The address was couched in courteous but resolute terms, pointing to the " many monstrous anomalies springing out of the constitution of society, the corruptions of government and the defective education of mankind " as the cause of the abnormal condition that the bulk of the nation were toiling slaves from birth till death, that the middle classes were racked with the curse of business distrust, few being spared from bankruptcy, and that but a trifling portion of the successful few could be found " free from the disease of sloth and cares of idleness and debauchery." The exclusive few —it was set out—used all their means to retain within their own circle all the legislative and executive powers in order to protect themselves against the wrath of the suffering multitudes and to perpetuate " their own despotic sway."

The economic suffering of the masses is directly attributed to the want of suffrage:

To this baneful source of exclusive political power may be traced the persecution of fanaticism, the feuds of superstition, and most of the wars and carnage which disgrace our history. To this pernicious origin may justly be attributed the unremitted toil and wretchedness of your Majesty's industrious people, together with most of the vices and crimes springing from poverty and ignorance, which in a country blessed by nature, enriched by art, and boasting of her progress and knowledge, mock her humanity and degrade her character. . . . These exclusive interests, under the names of Whig and Tory, have for many years past succeeded in making Royalty a mere puppet of their will. In that name they have plundered at home and desolated abroad. . . . But *the superstitious days of arbitrary dominion and holy errors are fast falling away;* the chief magistrate of an enlightened people must learn to know and respect its delegated authority—and must look for power and fame to the welfare of the people. . . . We trust that your Majesty will not permit either of the factions who live on abuses, and profit at the expense of the millions, to persuade you to any course of policy other than that of *right and justice.* . . . It is *not just,* that out of a population of *twenty-five millions of people,* only *eight hundred thousand* should have the power of electing what is called the Commons' House of Parliament.

The naive faith of the association in political reform as a panacea for all evil can be seen from the address, which was sent in 1837 to the American " brethren ", extolling the political liberty and institutions enjoyed by the workingmen in the United States, and at the same time conveying deep surprise at the fact that they had not progressed any further after sixty years of freedom: [1]

Why are you, to so great an extent, ruled by men who speculate on your credulity and thrive by your prejudices? Why have lawyers a preponderating influence in your country? . . . Why has so much of your fertile country been parcelled out between swindling bankers and grinding capitalists who seek to establish (as in our own country) a monopoly in that land which nature bestowed in common to all her children? Why have so many of your cities, towns, railroads, canals, and manufactories, become the monopolized property of those " who toil not, neither do they spin "?—while you, who raised them by your labors, are still in the position of begging leave to erect others, and to establish for them similar monopolies?

In the general election of 1837, the most outspoken Liber-

---

[1] Lovett, *op. cit.,* pp. 130, 131.

als, S. Crawford, Colonel Thompson and Roebuck, were defeated by the united opposition of the Whigs and Tories. Far from being discouraged, the London Working Men's Association called a meeting of the Committee of Twelve which had been appointed to prepare the bill. The committee then authorized Roebuck and Lovett to draft the document. With the exception of the preamble which was written by Roebuck, the bill was prepared by Lovett, after having consulted Francis Place as to its form and legal technicalities. The original draft contained a provision for the suffrage of women. This was discarded as it was feared that such demand might retard the suffrage of men. After some other changes were made, Lovett's Bill was finally approved by the Committee of Twelve and then by the London Working Men's Association. *This bill was designated the " People's Charter ".*[1] Daniel O'Connell, who before long deserted the ranks of the Chartists, virulent in his opposition till the day of his death, is credited with exclaiming, while handing the bill to Lovett, " There, Lovett, is your Charter; agitate for it, and never be content with anything else."

The People's Charter was published on the 8th of May, 1838, and was sent broadcast together with an address, which was signed by Henry Hetherington, Treasurer, and William Lovett, Secretary, and which contained a popular exposition of the principles of the Charter and the plan for obtaining it:

Having frequently stated the reasons for zealously espousing the great principles of reform, we have now endeavored to set them forth. We need not reiterate the facts and unrefuted arguments which have so often been stated and urged in their support. Suffice it to say, that we hold it *to be an*

---

[1] See Appendix B.

axiom in politics, that *self-government, by representation, is the only* just foundation of political power—the only true basis of constitutional rights—the only legitimate parent of good laws;—and we hold it as an indubitable truth that all government which is based on any other foundation, has a perpetual tendency to degenerate into anarchy or despotism; or to beget class and wealth idolatry on the one hand, or poverty and misery on the other.

While, however, we contend for the principle of self-government, we admit that laws will only be just in proportion as the people are enlightened; on this, socially and politically, the happiness of all must depend; but, as self-interest, unaccompanied by virtue, ever seeks its own exclusive benefit, so will the exclusive and privileged classes of society ever seek to perpetuate their power and to proscribe the enlightenment of the people. Hence we are induced to believe that the enlightenment of all will sooner emanate from the exercise of political power by all the people, than by their continuing to trust to the selfish government of the few.

A strong conviction of these truths, coupled as that conviction is with the belief that most of our political and social evils can be traced to *corrupt* and *exclusive legislation*, and that the remedy will be found in extending to the people at large the exercise of those rights now monopolized by a few, has induced us to make some exertions towards embodying our principles in the Charter.

We are the more inclined to take some practicable step in favor of reform, from the frequent disappointments the cause has experienced. We have heard eloquent effusions in favor of political equality from the hustings, and the senate-house, suddenly change into prudent reasonings on property and privileges, at the winning smile of the minister. We have seen depicted in glowing language bright patriotic promises of the future, which have left impressions on us more lasting than the perfidy or apostacy of the writers. . . .

The object we contemplate in the drawing up of this bill is to cause the Radicals of the kingdom to form, if possible, a

concentration of their principles in a practical form, upon
which they could be brought to unite, and to which they might
point, as *a Charter they are determined to obtain.*

We intend that copies of it shall be forwarded to all the
Working Men's Associations and to all Reform Associations
in the kingdom to which we can have access, and we hereby
call upon them, in the spirit of brotherhood, to examine, sug-
gest, and improve upon it, until it is so perfected as to meet, as
far as possible, with general approbation. When it is so far
improved, and has received their sanction, we intend that it
shall be presented to Parliament, and we trust that petitions
will not be wanting to show how far we are united in demanding its enactment. We hope, also, that electors and non-
electors will continue to make it the pledge of their candidates;
will seek to extend its circulation; talk over its principles; and
resolve that, as public opinion forced the Whig Reform Bill,
so in like manner shall this bill eventually become the law of
England. . . . .

The publication of the People's Charter gave a fresh impetus to the enthusiasm of the universal suffragists. The
best talents of the Working Men's Associations and other
radical societies joined in a gigantic effort to obtain the immediate enactment of the Charter. The vague and ambiguous phraseology of the London Working Men's Association
gave place to a determined expression of class consciousness.
The general press cautioned against the Chartist missionaries
who were branded as scoundrels, firebrands, plunderers,
knaves, and assassins. The people, however, paid little
heed to these warnings and eagerly demonstrated their
" general approbation " of the Charter in a series of grand
meetings and parades.

CHAPTER VII

THE LEADERS

THE years 1838 and 1839 were the most auspicious for the Chartist Movement. Instigated by the acute economic distress, the people were in the mood to follow almost anybody who could stimulate their indignation to activity. The leaders seemed to have realized this and vied with each other in their endeavors to gain the confidence of the working class. The response of the people, however, was too spontaneous, almost volcanic, to allow the establishment of any efficient and responsible organization. As in every mass movement, many a leader was swept off his feet in the whirlwind of universal protest against the existing régime. Instead of leading, they were made to follow, and, at best, to agitate. This for a time saved the ranks of the Chartists from complete disruption, although it was an open secret that there were " two parties in the Chartist ranks," and, what is more, that they had " different objects in view," that these two parties were " decidedly hostile to each other," and that no union could ever take place between the " honest or determined Chartists and the weak, vacillating and scheming Chartists." [1]

The most essential difference, which was of prime importance for the evolutionary period of the movement, lay in the mode of agitation. The People's Charter emanated, as we have seen, from the London Working Men's Association,

---

[1] *The London Democrat*, April 20, 1839.

whose leaders designed a policy of moral force, of education.
In its first address, the association marked its future task in
the following terms:

Who can foretell the great political and social advantages
that must accrue from the wide extension of societies of this
description acting up to their principles? Imagine the honest,
sober and reflecting portion of every town and village in the
kingdom linked together as a band of brothers, honestly resolved to investigate all subjects connected with their interests,
and to prepare their minds to combat with the errors and
enemies of society—setting an example of propriety to their
neighbors, and enjoying even in poverty a happy home. And
in proportion as home is made pleasant, by a cheerful and
intelligent partner, by dutiful children, and by means of comfort, which their knowledge has enabled them to snatch from
the ale-house, so are the bitters of life sweetened with happiness.

Think you a corrupt Government could perpetuate its exclusive and demoralizing influence amid a people thus united
and instructed? Could a vicious aristocracy find its servile
slaves to render homage to idleness and idolatry to the wealth
too often fraudulently exacted from industry? Could the
present gambling influence of money perpetuate the slavery of
the millions, for the gains or dissipation of the few? Could
corruption sit in the judgment seat—empty-headed importance in the senate—money-getting hypocrisy in the pulpit—
and debauchery, fanaticism, poverty, and crime stalk tri-
umphantly through the land—if the millions were educated in
a knowledge of their rights? No, no, friends; and hence the
efforts of the exclusive few to keep the people ignorant and
divided. Be ours the task, then, to unite and instruct them;
for be assured the good that is to be must be begun by ourselves.

At the beginning the agitation was preëminently peaceful.
The London Working Men's Association introduced a sys-

tem of national and international addresses as a means for
enlightening the people on all social and political events of
importance.   The addresses were well received by the better
elements of the working class, but failed to exert so great
an effect on the masses who felt impatient with the " moral,
vacillating, scheming humbugs," and preferred " to take
their affairs in their own hands."   It was no surprise, therefore, that the advocates of physical force and insurrection,
welcomed by the people from the very outset, soon gained
the upper hand in the movement.   Indeed, rampant dissatisfaction was displayed on more than one occasion, and
some of the leaders went even so far as to withdraw their
active support.   The fatal blight of discord was, however,
overcome during the first period.   The masses were imbued with the hope that the People's Charter would bring
about complete salvation.   The Charter contained, indeed,
only political reforms, but the people knew from the leaders that such reforms were the only instrument for the extermination of all evils.   The Chartist speakers, as well as
the Chartist writers, all agreed that the curse of the country
lay in " class legislation ":

It has corrupted the whole government—poisoned the press,
demoralized society, prostituted the Church, dissipated the resources of the nation, created monopolies, paralyzed trade,
ruined half its merchants, produced almost national bankruptcy, depressed the whole working classes, and pauperized
most of them.   Consequently, the sooner we get rid of such a
monstrous system, it will be so much the better for all, except for those who either live, or expect to live, by plunder.[1]

The masses believed, they were eager to believe in everything which held out the promise of relief.   They took up

[1] *The Chartist Circular*, April 18, 1840.

the rallying cry, "The Charter, the whole Charter, and
nothing but the Charter," with a zeal characteristic of the
common people. This reacted on the leaders and forced
their personal and theoretical differences to the background.
The differences were by no means given up. The leaders
merely buried their hatchets for a while, with the understanding that they would be picked up again at the oppor-
tune time after the Charter should have become an accom-
plished fact. Until then they were willing to let their economic and social creeds take care of themselves. This was
made clear by Bronterre even as early as 1837. In discussing his pet theory of nationalization of land, he cut himself
short:

Better, far better it were to sink such questions for the
present. When all shall have votes, it will be in the power of
each to make known his sentiments respecting the land, as well
as respecting everything else, and should a majority think with
him, his sentiments will become law without cavil or con-
straint. Till then, our theories, however just, are useless.[1]

The good intentions of the leaders were not realized.
There were too many points of friction in their mental constitution as well as in their temperamental make-up. At
the time of popular excitement, all were carried away by
the torrent of general indignation, few stopping to soothe
their personal feelings. It was only after the movement
had met the strenuous opposition on the part of the government and had become paralyzed, that demoralization set in,
disrupting the Chartist army into a number of hostile squads.
    The small coterie of leaders, who during the first period
stamped their personalities on the movement and directed
the destinies of millions of people, included men of excep-

[1] *The National Reformer*, Feb. 25, 1837.

tional character and mentality, who gave themselves like martyrs to the cause.

William Lovett, the author of the People's Charter and " the gentlest of agitators," was, according to the description of Francis Place, a tall, thin and rather melancholy man, " soured with the perplexities of the world," but " honest-hearted, possessed of great courage and persevering in his conduct." He was born on the 8th of May, 1800, in a little fishing town in the county of Cornwall. His father, a captain of a small trading vessel, was drowned before William was born. As a boy Lovett received some schooling in a rather suffocating religious atmosphere.

My poor mother, [he writes of his boyhood], like too many serious persons of the present day, thought that the great power that has formed the numerous gay, sportive, singing things of earth and air, must above all things be gratified with the solemn faces, prim clothes, and half sleepy demeanor of human beings ; and that true religion consists in listening to the reiterated story of man's fall, of God's anger for his doing so, of man's sinful nature, of the redemption, and of other questionable matters, instead of the wonders and glories of the universe.[1]

In his early youth, he was apprenticed to a rope-maker for a term of seven years. His master, however, soon gave up his indentures, and Lovett turned to fishing and other trades. On the 23rd of June 1821, he went to London where, after some struggles and adventures, he became a cabinet-maker. In 1828, he joined the " First London Coöperative Trading Association " and soon afterwards accepted the position of store-keeper in this association. He was also a prominent member of the " British Association for Promoting Coöperative Knowledge."

---

[1] William Lovett, *Life and Struggles*, pp. 7-8.

At that time he believed that the gradual accumulation of capital, by means of coöperative trading associations, might ultimately enable the working classes to get the industries and commerce of the country in their own hands. He also accepted Robert Owen's doctrine of community of property:

The idea of all the powers of machinery, of all the arts and inventions of men, being applied for the benefit of all in common, to the lightening of their toil and the increase of their comforts, is one the most captivating to those who accept the idea without investigation. The prospect of having spacious halls, gardens, libraries, and museums, at their command; of having light alternate labor in field or factory; of seeing their children educated, provided and cared for at the public expense; of having no fear or care of poverty themselves; nor for wife, children, or friends they might leave behind them; is one the most cheering and consolatory to an enthusiastic mind. I was one who accepted this grand idea of machinery working for the benefit of all.[1]

In 1830, he was active in the formation of the " Metropolitan Political Union," whose object was " to obtain by every just, legal, constitutional and peaceful means an effectual and radical reform in the Commons' House of Parliament." He was also connected with the "unstamped" agitation which originated the cheap political newspapers and pamphlets. In 1831, he refused to serve in the militia, as he explained it, " on the ground of not being represented in Parliament and of not having any voice or vote in the election of those persons who made those laws that compelled me to take up arms to protect the rights and property of others, while my *own rights* and the only property I had, *my labor*, were not protected." [2]   The same year, he joined "The National

---

[1] Lovett, *op. cit.*, pp. 43-44.
[2] *Ibid.*, p. 66.

Union of the Working Classes and Others," which declared labor the " source of wealth " and aimed at " the protection of the working men; the free disposal of the produce of labor; and effectual reform of the Commons' House of Parliament; the repeal of all bad laws; the enactment of a wise and comprehensive code of laws; and to collect and organize a peaceful expression of public opinion." This association, also known as the Rotundists, was denounced by the Tory and Whig press as consisting of " destructives, revolutionists, pickpockets, and incendiaries; meditating an attack upon every possessor of property, and the uprooting of all law and order." The rapid success of the Trades Unions in 1834, and especially of the Consolidated National Trades Union, led to the dissolution of the National Union of the Working Classes. After the trade union movement was crushed by the manufacturers and the government, Lovett, who enjoyed an enviable reputation among the London reformers, succeeded, together with a number of other radicals, in the effort to organize the London Working Men's Association. He had at that time renounced some of his ultra-radical ideas and adopted the policy of Francis Place, the wire-puller. He was an able organizer and, as its secretary, soon became the heart and soul of the association.

As the author of the People's Charter, Lovett undoubtedly exerted an influence on the movement. At no stage, however, was he regarded as a popular leader. For that he lacked both intellect and pliability. He was an idealist, ready to incur peril and obloquy for his principles, but his mentality was of a static nature. In all his Chartist career he never swerved from the path which the London Working Men's Association had laid out in 1836. Utterly incapable of being swayed by sentiment or emotion, he lacked completely the instinct and the foresight of a born leader.

Honest he was, indeed, and courageous, but it was the honesty and courage of a fanatic. He scrupled to yield to the popular clamor for physical force, but his scruples did not spring from the source of moral opulence. Obscured by men of greater power of leadership, he was ever full of suspicion and when forced to make some compromise, he begrudged it all his life. " His fault was," testifies one of his admirers, "that he had too much suspicion of the motives of others not taking his view of things." [1]   He was gentle and not spiteful, but he never bowed to anybody, nor allowed himself to be treated as a common mortal. His errors he attributed to the goodness of his heart and never to the weakness of his mind. Such was the make-up of the man who was considered by most writers the noblest exponent of the Chartist movement.

Feargus O'Connor was a man of a diametrically opposite calibre. Loved and worshipped by millions, hated by many, but despised by none, he was a man who could fairly say of himself : " It is my boast that neither the living denouncer nor the unborn historian can ever write of Chartism, leaving out the name of Feargus O'Connor." [2]   He was born July 16, 1794, and was the son of Roger O'Connor, who suffered imprisonment for his activity in the movement of the " United Irishmen." He was always proud of his descent which he traced to Roderick O'Connor, the last king of Ireland. He attended grammar-school and Trinity College at Dublin, but took no degree.

He was called to the Irish Bar, but lived with his brothers on their father's estate, and was, as he says, " on the turf in a small way." He appeared on the

---

[1] George Jacob Holyoake, *Sixty Years of an Agitator's Life*, London, 1900, vol. ii, p. 269.

[2] *The Laborer*, 1847, vol. i, p. 176.

political scene at the age of thirty-seven. A barrister by education, an orator of the first rank, and a man of athletic physical strength, he was a great prize for O'Connell's party in Ireland. He was elected to Parliament in 1833 for the County of Cork. While in Parliament, he repudiated the unscrupulous policy of his chief, Daniel O'Connell, who, on his part, could not brook anyone who was potentially fit to share his power or popularity. O'Connell frequently yielded to the Whigs with a view of securing a chance for his party. O'Connor denounced such tactics and frequently went out of his way to frustrate the plans of the Irish leader. He was re-elected in 1835, but was unseated owing to his want of the necessary property qualification. It was at that time that an open quarrel took place between him and O'Connell, who made " a present of him to the English radicals." The latter received him with open arms. Coming as he did from a family of famous Irish patriots, his name alone would have given great prestige to any radical group. But O'Connor possessed, in addition, a rich stock of personal qualifications for leadership. A giant of over six feet in height, with features which revealed great intellectual vigor, of aristocratic manner and deportment, his whole countenance was such as to strike awe into the masses. He was a man of unbounded energy and, after he was unseated in 1835, he selected the manufacturing districts for his agitation against the New Poor Law and the Factory System. On his tour he founded many political unions which ultimately associated themselves with the Chartists. It was on account of that tour that Francis Place characterized him as the *traveling leader* of the Democratic Movement. In 1836 he founded the Central Committee of radical unions. In 1837 he was wrought up by the invitation which the London Working Men's Association had extended to Daniel O'Connell as one

of the radical Parliamentary members,[1] and he denounced
the association for its alleged readiness to leave the interests
of the workingmen in the hands of the middle class. On
November 18, 1837, he founded the most radical Chartist
weekly, the *Northern Star*, whose circulation soon reached
sixty thousand. This unusual circulation testifies to the
great popularity which O'Connor enjoyed among the masses.
He was literally worshipped by his followers and many
"would have gone through fire and water for him."

There was much that was attractive in him when I first knew
him [writes one of the Chartists]. His fine manly form and
his powerful baritone voice gave him great advantage as a
popular leader. His conversation was rich in Irish humor,
and often evinced a shrewd knowledge of character. The fact
of his having been in the House of Commons, and among the
upper classes, also lent him influence. I do not think half a
dozen Chartists cared a fig about his boasted descent from
"Roderick O'Connor, the king of Connaught, and last king
of all Ireland"; but the connection of his family with the
United Irishmen and patriotic sufferers of the last century,
rendered him a natural representative of the cause of political
liberty.[2]

In his career as a Chartist, O'Connor displayed qualities
which, in the eyes of many contemporaries and historians,
branded him as a demagogue, a despot, a political denouncer,
a man who was looking solely for self-aggrandizement and
for personal interests. Lovett, who could hardly tolerate
the presence of O'Connor, once said to him, " You are the
great 'I am' of politics." Bronterre nicknamed him
"the dictator"; Roebuck called him "a cowardly and
malignant demagogue," "a rogue and a liar"; Place said

---

[1] *Cf. supra*, p. 90.

[2] *The Life of Thomas Cooper, written by himself*, London, 1897, p.
179.

of him that he would use every means he could to lead and
mislead the working people.   Historians, too, characterize
him as an empty braggart and a typical demagogue.   This
is as one-sided as it is unjust.   It was as natural for him
to " dictate ", as it was for others to follow.   It was his
great personality that impressed itself on others.   But he
was as large-hearted as any man could be.   He was, as he
himself testified, " of an enthusiastic and excitable disposition." [1]   At the same time he was the " most impetuous and
most patient of all the tribunes who ever led the English
Chartists." [2]   A born leader, he possessed great power of
reading the minds of the people and of designing his plans of
action according to conditions and circumstances.   This
often made him yield to popular clamor; but this is the lot
of every great leader who can feel the pulse of the masses.
He was vain and lacked modesty when speaking of himself;
but he was in no less a degree ready to exaggerate the
greatness of others.   He could with a sense of self-detach-
ment say of himself that he " led the people from madness
to sanity," as he could speak of Bronterre's " gigantic talents."   Holyoake acknowledges O'Connor's "great strength
of indifference to what any one of his rivals said against
him in his own columns of the Star." [3]   He had a deep
passion for freedom and, on more than one occasion and in
various forms of self-sacrifice, he proved his genuine devotion to the cause.   He was called the Lion of Freedom,
and the name was well merited.

During the first period of the Chartist agitation, O'Connor
cherished no special theories of his own.   His *Land Plan*
came at a later stage.   But even as early as 1835, he gave
notice of his intention to move in Parliament for leave to
bring in a bill

[1] See *English Chartist Circular*, vol. i, no. 36.
[2] See Holyoake, *op. cit.*, vol. i, p. 106.   [3] *Ibid.*, p. 107.

to compel landlords to make leases of their land in perpetuity—
that is, to give to the tenant a lease for ever, at a corn rent;
to take away the power of distraining for rent; and in all
cases where land was held upon lease and was too dear, that the
tenant in such cases should have the power of empaneling a
jury to assess the real value in the same manner as the crown
has the power of making an individual sell property required
for what is called public works or conveniences according to
the valuation of a jury.[1]

He believed that "the law of primogeniture is the eld-
est son of class legislation upon corruption by idleness."[2]
But unlike most of his Chartist colleagues, he was a strenuous opponent of the current Socialist theories.

I have ever been, and I think I ever shall be opposed to the
principles of *communism*, as advocated by several theorists.
I am, nevertheless, a strong advocate of co-operation, which
means legitimate exchange, and which circumstances would
compel individuals to adopt, to the extent that communism
would be beneficial. I have generally found that the strongest
advocates of communism are the most lazy members of society,—a class who would make a division of labor, adjudging
to the most pliant and submissive the lion's share of work,
and contending that their natural implement was the brain,
whilst that of the credulous was the spade, the plough, the
sledge and the pickaxe. Communism either destroys wholesome emulation and competition, or else it fixes too high a
price upon distinction, and must eventually end in the worst
description of despotism . . . whilst, upon the other hand, individual possession and coöperation of labor creates a wholesome bond between all classes of society.[3]

---

[1] *The English Chartist Circular*, vol. ii, no. 67.

[2] See Feargus O'Connor, *The Remedy for National Poverty Impend-
ing National Ruin*, 1841.

[3] *The Laborer*, 1847, vol. i, p. 149.

As land was, in his opinion, the only source of all wealth so was the unrestricted use of machinery the only source of all social evil:[1]

It opens a fictitious, unsettled, and unwholesome market for labor, leaving to the employer complete and entire control over wages and employment. As machinery becomes improved, manual labor is dispensed with, and the dismissed constitute a surplus population of unemployed, system-made paupers, which makes a reserve for the masters to fall back upon, as a means of reducing the price of labor. It makes character valueless. By the application of fictitious money, it overruns the world with produce, and makes labor a drug. It entices the agricultural laborer, under false pretences, from the natural and wholesome market, and locates him in an unhealthy atmosphere, where human beings herd together like swine. It destroys the value of real capital in the market, and is capable of affecting every trade, business, and interest, though apparently wholly unconnected with its ramifications. It creates a class of tyrants and a class of slaves. Its vast connection with banks, and all the moneyed interests of the country, gives to it an unjust, injurious, anomalous, and direct influence over the government of the country.

It was not, however, to the strength of his theories that O'Connor looked for recognition. It was his harangues against the New Poor Law and the Factory System that electrified the masses. Coming as he did in direct contact with the masses and witnessing their distress in all parts of the country, he was from the beginning of the Chartist movement inclined toward a revolutionary policy. To counterbalance the influence of the London Working Men's Association which, according to O'Connor, consisted of skilled mechanics, he founded in 1837 the London Demo-

[1] *The English Chartist Circular*, no. 62.

cratic Association, appealing to the "unshaven chins, blistered hands, and fustian jackets" for membership. The objects, besides universal suffrage, included the agitation for liberty of the press, the repeal of the Poor Law, an eight-hour labor day, and the prohibition of child labor. This association eventually became the mouthpiece of the physical force Chartists. disseminating the spirit of revolt all over the country. "In the Democratic Association", it was subsequently stated in its official organ, "the Jacobin Club again lives and flourishes, and the villainous tyrants shall find to their cost, that England too has her Marats, St. Justs, and Robespierres ".[1] O'Connor, however, never identified himself with the extreme wing of the terrorists and once he even repudiated the latter in his characteristic vein. [2]

I have always been a man of peace. I have always denounced the man who strove to tamper with an oppressed people by any appeal to physical force. I have always said that moral force was the degree of deliberation in each man's mind which told him when submission was a duty or resistance not a crime ; and that a true application of moral force would effect every change, but that in case it should fail, physical force would come to its aid like an electric shock—and no man could prevent it ; but that he who advised or attempted to marshal it would be the first to desert it at the moment of danger. God forbid that I should wish to see my country plunged into the horrors of physical revolution. I wish her to win her liberties by peaceful means alone.

His apprehension of a "physical revolution" did not, nevertheless, in the least mitigate his contempt for those who counseled inactivity and "education". He fully realized

[1] *The London Democrat*, no. 2, 1839.
[2] *The Nonconformist*, June 8, 1842.

that there were two parties to the bargain; that, besides the poor fellow, there was also the rich man who was reluctant to be "educated" in detriment to his personal interests. In his speeches, as well as in his "Star," he repeatedly upbraided the people for having borne oppression too long and too tamely, reminding them that "it is better to die free men than to live slaves." Professing his faith in the moral power of the working class to establish *the rights of the poor man*, he used his intrepid eloquence and sallies of wit to bring the masses to the very pit of revolution.

James Bronterre O'Brien, widely known as Bronterre, was born in 1805 and was the son of a wine merchant and tobacco manufacturer. In childhood he displayed extraordinary abilities and, at the age of ten, he knew Latin, Greek, French and Italian, besides his native language. In the private school which was conducted by Lowell Edgeworth, a brother of the writer, on the monitor system, he showed remarkable proficiency in mathematics and a fine appreciation of literature and poetry. Walter Scott, who had heard of the boy-prodigy, went to see him in school and was filled with admiration. He also distinguished himself in Trinity College at Dublin, where he received the degree of Bachelor of Arts, and at Gray's Inn in London where he was qualifying himself for the bar. He was twenty-five years of age when he was introduced by "Orator" Henry Hunt to the radicals of London as a young gentleman of great abilities, whose sympathies were entirely with the people. In the account which he gave of himself in the first number of his "National Reformer," January 7, 1837, he says:

About eight years ago, I came to London to study law and radical reform. My friends sent me to study law; I took to radical reform on my own account. I was a very short time engaged in both studies, when I found the law was all fiction and rascality, and that radical reform was all truth and matter of dire necessity. Having a natural love of truth, and as natural a hatred of falsehood, I soon got sick of law, and gave all my soul to radical reform. The consequence is, that while I have made no progress at all in law, I have made immense progress in radical reform, so much so, that were a professorship of radical reform to be instituted in King's College, I think I would stand candidate for the office. At all events, I feel as though every drop of blood in my veins was radical blood, and as if the very food I swallow undergoes, at the moment of deglutition, a process of radicalization.

He started his literary career in 1830, over the signature of Bronterre, in *Carpenter's Political Pamphlets*. His articles soon attracted the attention of the radicals, and, at the age of twenty-six, he became the chief editor of the *Poor Man's Guardian*. He was a prolific writer and during the thirties was an important contributor or editor of many magazines, including the *Midland Representative, People's Conservative, Carpenter's Political Pamphlets* and *Political Herald, Poor Man's Guardian, The Destructive, Twopenny Despatch, London Mercury, National Reformer, The Operative, Southern Star, Northern Star*, and others. In 1836 he translated Buonarroti's *History of Babeuf's Conspiracy for Equality*, and, after his visit to Paris, published, in 1837, *The Life of Robespierre*, in which, in defiance of all prejudice, he depicted the great revolutionist as one of the noblest and most enlightened reformers that the world ever had. He remained all his life a great admirer of Robespierre and Babeuf.

The talents of Bronterre were greatly exaggerated by many of his followers, who ranked him as a genius, but they were great enough to put him head and shoulders above the average leader of workingmen. The title of " School

Master" bestowed on him for his learning by O'Connor was fully merited. As a leader, he combined many happy characteristics. He was a dreamer and full of temperament. less erratic than O'Connor and more pliant than Lovett. Tall, somewhat stooping, with a fine intellectual cast of head and features, forcible with his tongue not less than with his pen, he exerted a great influence on the masses as well as on the leaders. The goal which he set out to achieve was " social equality for each and all." But in order to obtain *social* equality, the people had first to get *political* equality. Political supremacy was the foundation of the whole economic structure. Social theories were, therefore, " useless " until the Charter became the law of the land. At the beginning of his radical career he referred to the Houses of Parliament in the following terms: [1]

They might abolish or remodel every institution in Church and State; they might change the whole system of commerce; they might substitute the labor note for the present vicious currency and thus render usury impossible; they might agree to work in common, and to enjoy in common; or they might arrange to exchange their produce on equitable terms, through salaried agents, without the intervention of base middlemen who are the bane of society. By these and the like means they might silently, but effectually, regenerate the world.

This view was elaborated by Bronterre in his writings during the Chartist agitation. The acquisition of universal suffrage was, therefore, imperative in order that the working class may reconstruct the whole basis of society. This became his *idée fixe*:

Without the franchise you can have nothing but what others choose to give you, and those who give to-day, may choose to

---

[1] *The Poor Man's Guardian*, March 1, 1834.

take away to-morrow. Every industrious man who produces more (in value) of the goods of life than he needs for his own or his family's use, ought to own the difference as property. You are almost all in that condition, for there are few of you who do not yield more value to society every day than society gives you back in return. Why are you not masters of the difference? Why is it not your property? Because certain laws and institutions, which other people make, take it away from you, and give it to the law-makers. But if *you* were represented as well as *they*, you would have quite other laws and institutions, which would give the wealth to those who earned it.[1]

Bronterre was an ardent advocate of nationalization of land. In 1837 he advanced the basic points which he subsequently developed into a theory of his own:

1. The absolute dominion, or allodial right to the soil, belongs to the nation only.
2. The nation alone has the just power of leasing out the land for cultivation, and of appropriating the rents accruing therefrom.
3. The size of farms, or the portion of soil to be allotted to individuals or families; also the proportions to be devoted to tillage, pasturage, *etc.*—also the several other powers now possessed by individual owners, and exercised by them in the granting of leases, *etc.*—all these are matters which it also belongs to the nation alone to determine in virtue of its rights as absolute landlord of all.
4. Upon this theory every subject of the realm is a part proprietor of the soil. The land being leased out by public auction, whoever bids highest for a lot should get it, because the nation would thereby be the gainer, and as population increased, and the land became in consequence more valuable, rents would increase also, and people's inheritance be made greater.[2]

[1] Bronterre's *National Reformer*, January 15, 1837.
[2] *Ibid.*, Feb. 25, 1837.

His hostility towards the middle class, the "money-monster", did not entirely blind him to the advantages of machinery. Nor did he believe with O'Connor that land was the *only* source of *all* wealth:

The system I combat, and which I wish you to combat, is *that* by which your profit-mongering oppressors have turned you from agriculturists into manufacturers for all the world. Now, I am not against manufactures, nor against the fine arts, nor against even the largest possible extension and application of both to the purpose of human economy, but I am against the system which would first make these paramount to agriculture, and then bestow all the advantages of both on an upstart moneyed aristocracy, who, in drawing you from off the land, have made you more abject slaves to their cupidity, than your forefathers ever were to the feudal barons of the Middle Ages. Agriculture is the most profitable of all pursuits, to a nation considered aggregately; even now, when scarcely any machinery is applied to husbandry, it is a well known fact that one laborer produces food for *four* persons. How much more he might produce, I leave any one to infer, who has ever seen the rich garden grounds about Chelsea, Fulham, Kensington, and Hammersmith. Is it not monstrous, then, that with this power of production, and with sixty millions of acres of land in Great Britain and Ireland, of which not ten millions are unsusceptible of cultivation, we should see thousands of artisans in our great towns, either wholly destitute of employment, or eking out a miserable existence on starving wages, and subject to all the brutalizing privations of health, air, and happiness, to which their dependence on the profit-monger and his foreign markets hourly subjects them? . . . It is not gold and silver, nor yet bank notes, as the paper-money schemers would have us believe, that have given the prodigious impulse we have witnessed, to improvements in America. It is the abundance of food produced by its agricultural population, that enables so great a number to be employed in constructing canals, bridges, railroads, etc. The surplus of agricultural produce is the *real capital* which sets the artisans and handi-craftsmen to work, and covers the States with those embellishments and stupendous works of art which astound the European traveler.[1]

It was observations like the above that led him to conclude that land could never be a "legitimate subject of property", and that had it not been for individual ownership of land, "we should have escaped ninety-nine hundredths of all the woes and crimes that have hitherto made a pandemonium of the world."[2]   He put land in a class by itself.   All other property could be held by individuals in perfect compatibility with public happiness and social justice.

If all men are placed equal before the law—if the means of acquiring and retaining wealth are equally secured to all in proportion to the respective industry and services of each, I see no objection to private property.   Every man has a right to the value of his own produce or services, be they more or less.   If one man can and will do twice the work of another man, he ought certainly in justice to have twice the reward. But if his superior strength or skill gives him the means of acquiring more wealth than his neighbor, it by no means follows that he ought, therefore, to acquire a right or power over his neighbor's produce as well as his own.   And here lies the grand evil of society—it is not in private property, but in the unjust and atrocious powers with which the existing laws of all countries invest it.   If a man has fairly earned a hundred or a thousand pound's worth of wealth beyond what he has consumed or spent, he has a sacred right to the exclusive use of it, if he thinks proper; but he has no right to use that wealth in such a way as to make it a sort of sucking pump, or thumb-screw for sucking and screwing other

[1] Bronterre's *National Reformer*, January 7, 1837.
[2] *The Operative*, vol. i, no. 4, 1838.

people's produce into his possession.   Sir John Cam Hobhouse, for example, . . . has no just right to employ his money in usury or speculation.   His money should not be allowed to grow money as cabbage grows cabbage, or weeds grow weeds. To employ money in that way is not to use the right of property, but to practice robbery. . . . He takes advantage of his 'capital,' and the poverty that surrounds him.   He says to the hungry man, Come and labor for me, create fresh wealth for me, and you shall have a small share of your produce to keep you alive. . . . The laborer can stand anything before hunger.   Hence, Sir John grows richer and richer every day, without earning any riches at all, while he who produces the riches grows poorer and poorer, as age diminishes his strength, till at last he dies in poverty and in the workhouse. . . . The *employers* of labor and the *exchangers* of wealth are alone considered in the laws.   The *producers* and active distributors are only thought of as slaves or criminals.   Enormous fleets and armies are kept up to protect the merchant's gains.   Enormous gaols and penitentiaries are kept up for the poor.   Thus are the laborers forced to pay, not only for the protection of those who plunder them, but for the very instruments of their own torture and misery.   Buonarroti considers all these results inseparable from private property.   So did Babeuf—so did thousands of the French Democrats of 1793—so do Robert Owen and his disciples of the present day.   I think differently.   I will never admit that private property is incompatible with public happiness, till I see it fairly tried.   I never found an objection urged against it, which I can not trace to the *abuse,* not to the *use* of the institution. . . . I assert that such [enlightened] government would place commerce and manufactures upon a totally different footing from the present, and make the land the common property of all the inhabitants, and that, without any real or material injury to the existing proprietors.   I hold, and I am sure I can prove, that such a dispensation of things is within the power of an enlightened legislature, fairly representing all classes.[1]

[1] *The English Chartist Circular,* vol. i, no. 18.

Radical and talented as Bronterre was, his strong predilections for the views of Robespierre and Babeuf entirely
blurred his vision of the evolutionary laws of society.   In
the preface to his translation of Buonarroti's *History of
Babeuf's Conspiracy for Equality*, he cites, among others,
the following reasons for rendering the work into English.

Because Buonarroti's book contains one of the best exposi-
tions I have seen of those great political and social principles
which I have so long advocated in the *Poor Man's Guardian*
and other publications. . . . Society has been hitherto constituted upon no fixed principles.   The state in which we find
it is the *blind result of chance.*   Even its advocates do not
claim for it any other origin.   The right of the strongest—
the only right acknowledged by savage man—appears to be
still the fundamental charter of all " civilized " states. . . . .
What the savage or uncivilized man does *individually* and
directly by the exercise of mere personal prowess, the civilized
man (so called) does *collectively* and circuitously by cunningly-
designed institutions.   The effects of these institutions are
well depicted by Buonarroti.   He shows, with admirable ability, how, in trying to escape the evils of savage life, man has
unconsciously plunged into another state far more calamitous
—to wit, the present artificial state, which he terms that of
" false civilization."   He shows, that to correct the evils of
this latter state, without at the same time retrograding to the
former, was the grand problem sought to be resolved by the
first French Revolution, and, in discussing the principles and
institutions deemed necessary to that end by the leaders of
the Revolution, I was so forcibly struck by the coincidence
of Buonarroti's ideas with my own, that I immediately resolved to translate the book.

The omnipotence which he attributed to political rights
precluded his correct appreciation of the economic forces
of society.   The rise of the middle class forced his recognition, but he ascribed it to the political importance of that

class, which in his mind was merely "the blind result of chance," and he sought to crush the "money-monster" with its own weapon—political power. In this respect he was in full accord with Lovett and his friends of the London Working Men's Association, never tiring of agitating for universal suffrage as the only remedy for social maladies. The economic rôle of the working class as a factor in social evolution he neither recognized nor understood.

Thomas Attwood was a valuable accession to the Chartist leaders on account of his previous association with the Birmingham Political Union. He was a Birmingham banker, and his interest in currency reform led him into active politics. At the beginning of his political career, he looked with contempt upon the "poor wretches," the radicals, who "clamor for Burdett and liberty meaning blood and anarchy." After the defeat of his currency measures in Parliament, he proclaimed himself a radical reformer, and in December, 1829, together with fourteen others, he founded the "Birmingham Political Union for the Protection of Public Rights" and rendered yeoman's service in the agitation for the Reform Bill of 1832. He was extremely popular among all classes, and, as a politician, he adopted a somewhat modern method of gaining support by kissing the children and very often bestowing this token of recognition upon the mothers of the children. At one election he was credited to have kissed about eight thousand women. Among the Chartists, he belonged to the moral-force group.

As the leader of the Birmingham Currency School, he attributed every trouble which befell England to the resumption of specie-payment in 1819 and advocated the inflation of the currency by means of paper money, whose standard should be regulated in accordance with fluctuating prices. His pamphlets on monetary questions made him widely known, although he met with little sympathy in Parliamentary circles as well as among the radicals. Disraeli described him as a provincial banker laboring under a financial monomania. Cobbett accused him of desiring to keep up " an army deadweight, sinecures, places and pensions, the Stock Exchange in full swing and the infamous borough-mongers in the height of prosperity." O'Connor used to call his financial schemes " rag-botheration." An official declaration of the Chartists referred to the " corrupting influence of paper money " as the most " oppressive measure," by which the workingmen were " enslaved ".[1] Attwood, however, never tired of his agitation in favor of paper currency and worked the hardest for the People's Charter, harboring the belief that an ideal monetary reform would be enacted by a democratic Parliament.

Henry Hetherington was another man whose great popularity lent considerable support to the moral-force group of Chartists. He was not an orator of any force or eloquence, but enjoyed an enviable reputation as the champion and martyr of the battle for an unstamped press. Prisons had no terrors for him, and for a period of five years[2] he published the *Poor Man's Guardian* in open "defiance of *law* to try the power of *right* against *might*." In 1836 his *Twopenny Despatch* took the lead in the courageous struggle for a free and popular press. After the formation of the London Working Men's Association he was one of the missionaries who were sent out to organize similar bodies all over the country. As a Chartist he professed intimate sympathy with the principles and policies of his friend Lovett.

[1] See Hansard, vol. xlix, 1839, p. 242; *cf.* also Bronterre's view, *supra*, p. 116.

[2] Dec. 25, 1830, to Dec. 20, 1835.

CHAPTER VIII

> I am here to blow to the uttermost ends of the earth that lie—the impious and blasphemous lie of the hirelings—that you are bound to obey laws without knowing what they are. . . . Nothing can be more wicked or diabolical than that. Before you obey a law, you must know whether it is good or bad.
> —*Rev. J. R. Stephens.*

The Gospel of Revolt

WILLIAM LOVETT was the apostle of *Moral Force.* He had unbounded faith in the moral propensities of mankind. Since ignorance alone was at the root of all oppression, it was necessary only to awaken the dormant faculties of mind in order to assure the blissful regeneration of society. It was natural, then, that he should inspire the London Working Men's Association not to " rely on the mere excitation of the multitude to condemn bad men or measures, or to change one despot for another." No force other than moral suasion, backed by political and social education, would enable the people " to found their institutions on principles of equality, truth, and justice." [1]

O'Connor and Bronterre made no religion of *Moral Force.* They advocated "Peace and Order" not as a maxim, but as a policy. When the temper of the people dictated a different policy, they did not contradict it,—they

---

[1] See "Address to the Working Classes of Europe, and especially to the Polish People," in *Life and Struggles of William Lovett,* pp. 150-158.

did not even apologize,—they simply yielded to the inevitable. *Physical Force* as a philosophy and *Revolt* as an apotheosis of justice were broached by a different set of men who exerted a dominant influence on the masses during the first period of the movement.

Joseph Raynor Stephens, the apostle of revolt and the only Chartist who at one time vied with O'Connor in popularity, was born on the 18th of March, 1805, at Edinburgh, where his father was a Methodist preacher. He made the best of his elementary education when yet quite young. After teaching school for two years, he became a Methodist preacher in 1825, and the following year was appointed to a mission station at Stockholm, Sweden. In 1829 he was ordained as a Wesleyan minister and in 1830 was stationed at Cheltenham. His Wesleyan career ended in 1834, when he was dismissed for his association with Richard Oastler in the agitation for the improvement of the condition of factory laborers. The dismissal from the ministry raised him in the estimation of the working men. But it was his subsequent scathing attacks on the New Poor Law that endeared him to the masses who before long erected for him three chapels in the Ashton district. Besides his regular sermons in the chapels, he made use of the public market to harangue big crowds and to teach them not to " care for an Act of Parliament ", as it was only " waste paper ", " treason ", and " blasphemy ", unless it tended to promote happiness among men. He was never shy in the choice of his epithets against the ruling classes, and it was for this that Francis Place characterized him as a " malignant, crazy man who never seemed exhausted with bawling atrocious matter."

Stephens did not consider himself a radical, but, as " a revolutionist by fire, a revolutionist by blood, to the knife, to the death," be joined the ranks of the Chartists, proclaiming the question of universal suffrage to be, after all, " a knife and fork question." [1]   He was recognized as the greatest Chartist orator.   A master on the platform, he possessed personal magnetism, felicity of expression and a singular style of oratory which, at his best, made him irresistible.   Vehement inflammatory declamations interwoven with passages of classical beauty; rugged expressions of protest mingled with sentiments of love and devotion; scenes of revolting despondency redeemed by prophetic promises of a happy life; curses sputtered in a voice that could be distinctly heard by twenty thousand persons in the open air soothed by intonations of musical cadence; stories of every-day life, so near and familiar, followed by strange but exalted citations from the Bible,—all this rendered his spell the more dominant because of the spectacular effect produced by the black robe of a minister of the gospel.   His sermons were partly religious and partly political, but in all he exposed the crying injustice of the economic system. His pictures of women bleeding to death from overwork in factories, of children in mortal terror of the workhouse, of old men and old women dying from starvation, produced a lurid effect on the minds of his hearers and made them the more susceptible to his subtle allusions to force.   He made extensive use of the gospel to popularize his philosophy of social justice.   He preached class consciousness and organization as he preached religion.   He urged insurrection as he extolled the names of the Prophets.   He inspired courage in emulation of Christ:

Oh, my brethren, look neither to this man nor to that man, but pray to God Almighty to raise up among you prophets like unto Moses and Joshua and Hezekiah and Ezekiel and Mala-

[1] See *Annual Register*, vol. lxxx, 1839, p. 311.

chi, and Amos and Jonah; pray to God to raise up apostles like Peter and Paul and John; pray God to raise up men filled with his favor; men whose hearts are filled with love to their brethren; pray God to send such men out, with their lives in their hands, to launch his thunderbolts at the head of the oppressor, and to shed his blessing upon the heads of those who in obedience, reverential, child-like obedience, love to follow in the way of his commandments.

You will never have freedom or happiness in England; this land will never be worth living in—it is not worth living in now, if it were not for the hope in God that it may be better; if there be a hell upon earth comparatively with other nations of the world, it is England; if the devil has any seat of authority—any kingdom where he rules more infernally than in any other part of the world, it is England at this moment. Look where you will; cast your eyes abroad from the political head to the political foot, there is no soundness in us; there is nothing "but wounds and bruises, and putrifying sores," and the only balm of Gilead, the only good physician is yonder Good Physician—he who laid down his life for the world. Pray, then, for the spirit of God to be poured out; pray for the spirit of God to come down; pray for the spirit of determined and decided men once more to be imparted . . . ; pray that God would fill you with his truth, that he would raise you up and carry you far beyond the fear of man; and when your own soul is let loose, when your own mind is free, when your own heart is big and swollen, and entirely filled with the fear of God, you will never be afraid of what men can say or do unto you. You will say, "He that is for me, is greater than all that are against me"; and you will go on in the name. and in the strength of God, and you will be a Christian Reformer. We want in England Christian Reformers.[1]

Resistance to bad laws is, according to Stephens, as

[1] *A Sermon Preached at Hyde, in Lancashire, on the 17th of February, 1839.*

exalted a virtue as is obedience to good laws.   Allegiance
per se is not an end; if the law affords no protection, it
must be disobeyed.   His appeal for rebellion was direct:

Are the Spitalfields weavers protected, when not one in a hundred of them, after working twelve hours a day, can earn 12s.
a week?   Are the handloom weavers of the north protected,
when they cannot, with all their toil, earn more than 7s. a week?
I have known girls eight years of age working at the anvil, making nails from six in the morning until eight or nine at night,
and on Friday all night long, and, after all, could not earn
more than 1s. 6d. per week.   The mother worked equal time,
and whilst she was at work, one of her children was burnt
almost to a cinder, and she could only earn 3s. a week, whilst
the grandmother could get no more than 1s. 6d.   Do those
poor creatures owe *allegiance* to the laws?   Are they *protected?*   Do the poor wretches of the factories—the carders,
the piecers, the scavengers, dressers, weavers, and spinners
—do they owe allegiance to the laws?   Does the agricultural
laborer, who can only earn 8s. a week, owe submission to the
laws?   The law, in establishing oppression, makes the oppressed its deadly enemy.[1]

Stephens dwelt little on the political aspects of the Charter.   He aimed chiefly to impress the masses with the
realization of the iniquitous economic and social system.
" You see yonder factory with its towering chimney.   Every
brick in that factory is cemented with the blood of women
and little children ",—he said on one occasion.   He always
warned his hearers against passiveness.   On January 1,
1838, referring to the New Poor Law, he admonished a
Newcastle audience that " sooner than wife and husband,
and father and son, should be sundered and dungeoned. and

[1] *A Sermon Preached in Shepherd and Shepherdess Fields, London,
on Sunday, May 12, 1839.*

fed on ' skillee ', — sooner than wife or daughter should wear the prison dress—sooner than that—Newcastle ought to be, and should be—one blaze of fire, with only one way to put it out, and that with the blood of all who supported this abominable measure." He recurred to this theme in most of his sermons, and once he declared tersely :

I have never acknowledged the authority of the New Poor Law, and so help me God I never will. I never paid my rates under it, and so help me God I never will—they may take every chair, every table and every bed I have—they may pull my house over my head, and send me and my wife and my child wanderers on the heaths and the hills—they may take all but my wife, my child, and my life, but pay one penny I never will. If they dare attempt to take them, and it becomes necessary to repel force by force, there will be a knife, a pike, or a bullet at hand, and if I am to fall, I will at least sell life for life. I exhort you and all others to do the same. I do not mean to flinch. I will recommend nothing which I will not do. I tell you that if they attempt to carry into effect this *damnable law, I mean to fight.* I will lay aside the black coat for the red, and with the Bible in one hand and a sword in the other— a sword of steel, not of argument—I will fight to the death sooner than that law shall be brought into operation on me or on others with my consent or through my silence. . . . . Perish trade and manufacture — perish arts, literature and science—perish palace, throne and altar—if they can only stand upon the dissolution of the marriage tie—the annihilation of every domestic affection, and the vilest and most brutal oppression ever yet practiced upon the poor of any country in the world.[1]

The most salient feature in his sermons, besides their inciting character, was the subjection of politics to eco-

---

[1] *A Sermon Preached at Primrose Hill, London, on Sunday, May 12, 1839.*

nomic ends. Contrary to well-nigh all Chartists, he never made *universal suffrage* synonymous with *universal happiness.* He believed that every man without a home, or whose home was "not all that God meant it to be," was robbed and had, therefore, " a just cause for quarrel with society." [1] He gave his allegiance to the People's Charter in so far as it aimed to assure a *happy home* for every man " that breathed God's free air or trod God's free earth." But at the same time he realized, and endeavored to make the people realize that the Charter would be of no avail without a strong, organized, revolutionary movement for the purpose of effecting a complete change in the economic system:

There has already been too much of what is called political reform, the juggling of the places from one to another, the passing of the pea from one cup to another cup to amuse and to deceive, and ultimately to destroy the people; and every step you take is a step nearer to hell. *All the laws in England could not make Hyde one bit the better* unless the people were a changed people. An Act of Parliament cannot change the hearts of the tyrants Ashton and Howard. These men have made themselves rich by making you poor. They have swollen with wealth by plundering you. Now, all the laws in England could not change the hearts of those wicked men; and unless their hearts were changed, and your hearts were changed, what could the law do? There would be a thousand ways of breaking through it; a thousand ways of avoiding it and of screening those who were detected, even after they had broken the law. It could do no good. Your minds must be made up. You, husbands! unless your minds be made up that your wives ought not and shall not work; that rather than kill your wives by allowing them to work, you will allow God to take their lives by gradual starvation. . . . But God Almighty

[1] *A Sermon Preached in Shepherd and Shepherdess Fields, London, on Sunday, May 12, 1839.*

is moving the working classes in the country, and therefore I exhort you to give yourself to prayer. Pray God to sound the alarm from one end of the land to the other; and then, in the spirit of self-denial, and self-sacrifice, and devotion, be united as the heart of one man, and as one united and indissoluble phalanx, God leading you by a pillar of fire by night, and by a pillar of cloud by day, wend your way and force your passage through the wilderness of the promised land—the land that flows with milk and honey. It is high time there was some mighty movement.[1]

The emphasis which Stephens always laid on the economic aspects of the movement, not less than his advocacy of physical force, precluded Lovett and his friends from recognizing him as a *bona fide* Chartist. In an *Address to the Irish People*, published in August, 1838, in reply to the Precursors, the London Working Men's Association disclaimed all affiliation with Stephens, who was labeled as a man " more known for his opposition to the New Poor Law than for his advocacy of Radicalism ", and who " ridiculed our principles and publicly declared his want of confidence in us." [2]   His sermons support the suspicion that in his heart of hearts he probably never believed in the efficacy of political agitation. It may have been the vanity of a popular idol and the fear of losing his grip on the people that restrained him from speaking his mind; he may have felt reluctant to disillusion the masses in their faith in the talismanic power of the Charter; he may have himself been unconsciously caught in the maelstrom of universal agitation, or he may have cast his lot with the Chartists simply because the new movement afforded a wide field for the dissemination of his revolutionary ideas. At any rate, his

---

[1] *A Sermon Preached at Hyde, in Lancashire, on the 17th of February, 1839.*

[2] William Lovett, *Life and Struggles*, p. 195.

skepticism became the more pronounced the sterner the government became in its hostility towards the movement. In a sermon preached at Ashton on May 26th, 1839, he warned the people of the futility of abortive demonstrations and desultory fighting and advised them to divide themselves into little bands of five or ten in a company and to meet at each other's houses, and " there over the hearthstone, without books and papers, without speeches and resolutions, without anything but talking and praying, tell one another what they think, and ask one another whether they are right, and whether their minds are made up to shed the last drop of blood rather than live in bondage, and sell their wives and children to the devil." And then in an ebullition of indignation, he cried out:

Down with the House of Commons; down with the House of Lords; aye, down with the throne, and down with the altar itself; burn the church; down with all rank, all dignity, all title, all power; unless that dignity, authority, and power will and do secure to the honest industrious efforts of the upright and poor man a comfortable maintenance in exchange for his labor. *I don't care about your Charter;* it may be all very right; it may be all very good; you have a right to get it, mind you, and I will stand by you in it; but I don't care about it; and I don't care about a republic. You have a right to have it if you choose; and I will stand by you, in defending your right to have it if you choose. I don't care about a monarchy; I don't care about the present, or any other order of things, unless the Charter, the republic, the monarchy, the present order of things, or any other order of things that may be brought to succeed the present, should, first of all, and above all, and through all, secure to every son of the soil to every living being of the human kind . . . . a full, a sufficient and a comfortable maintenance, according to the will and commandment of God. That is what I go for; that is what I talk for; that is what I live for; and that is what

I will die for: for I will have it. I say now what I said
before; the earth is the Lord's, and the fullness thereof; the
cattle upon a thousand hills; the gold and the silver; and he
has filled all things with plenteousness. There is nothing nig-
gardly from God. There has nothing come in stinging, close-
fisted niggardliness from God Almighty. It is all plenty.
There is plenty of soil—there is plenty of water—there is
plenty of sun—there is plenty of rain—there is plenty of dew
—the winter throws a warm blanket of driven snow upon
the earth, to cover it and keep it warm: then He sends out
the sun to rule the day—refreshing and reviving is the breeze.
. . . What have we to thank God for? What have we to
bless God for? Does God call upon us to thank Him for
nothing? Then what kind of a God is He? And what sort
of worshippers does He take us to be? Does He call upon
us to bless Him for curses? Then what kind of a Maker,
Preserver, and Redeemer, and Judge, is He; and what kind of
workmanship of his Almighty hand are we? No, my brethren,
the very thought of such a thing is impiety and blasphemy;
God does not ask us to thank Him for nothing; or to bless
Him for curses. Then what have we to thank and bless God
for? You have to thank and bless God for houses and for
lands, for food and for clothing, which He has given you,
but which others have taken from you. . . . I thank God,
who gave me life and breath, and all things richly to enjoy.
And if any man asks me where they are, as a laboring man,
I answer, "God gave them, but wicked men have taken them
from me." But I not only thank God for having given
them to me; I not only bless God for having bestowed them
upon me, but I trust in God for strength to help me to take
them back again. I am alive, and therefore, I thank God, I
have the use of my understanding, and the understanding
shows me not only what things are, but what things ought to
be—and I trust that God, who gave me life, and who still lends
me breath, and intrusts me with power of body as well as
power of mind—I trust in that God, and I pray to that God,
that he would, if it be found that my rights cannot be got back

without it, and by any way short of it, " I pray God literally to teach my hands to war, and my fingers to fight." . . . . I preach a startling truth; I preach a sweeping truth; I preach the truth, which will, if they choose to suffer it, set things right, without hurting any body. If they will not suffer the truth— if they will neither have it, nor forbear from hindering it, then I preach a truth which will be the means, I hope, of destroying them root and branch. It is time the prisoners were let loose; it is time the dungeon was broken open; it is time the Bastile was burnt down; it is time that every working-man in England had the means, and there are the means, and they are not far off him, and the Government is beginning to find it out, and is arming the pensioners; but, unluckily for the devils who arm the pensioners, the pensioners are training the people. . . . You have a right, every working man amongst you has the right to as much for your labor as will keep you and your families.[1]

For some time the idol of the masses, Stephens, however, lost his influence as soon as his criticism of the Chartist demands became pronounced. It was his heresy in politics that drove him to the Chartists and it was the same heresy that barred him from their ranks. The chief protagonist and pillar of insurrectionism, he was the first to be singled out for persecution by the government and to be denounced by the leaders of the movement. The cult of physical force, however, always had more than one high priest.

George Julian Harney, unlike Stephens, devoted his ubiquitous activity to the exclusive agitation for the Charter. He was but twenty years of age when he plunged into the tempestuous sea of the Chartist movement. He came with a halo of martyrdom, having suffered imprisonment, when yet quite a boy, for selling unstamped literature. Brought up

---

[1] *The London Democrat*, June 8, 1839.

under extremely adverse circumstances, he cultivated a
feeling of antagonism towards the powers that be.   He
could not boast of a thorough education, but he possessed
great natural abilities.   He was the man who better than any
other of the Chartist leaders could in time read the handwriting on the wall, displaying a deep understanding of the
social fabric and a keen insight into the rôle which the working class was destined to play.   In many of his writings, he
foreshadowed the subsequent principles of scientific Socialism.   At the beginning of his career, however, he was the
most violent agitator of physical force.   He was the secretary of the " London Democratic Association " and, at the
age of twenty-two, was the chief writer for *The London
Democrat* which was started on the 13th of April, 1839, to
preach the gospel of insurrection.   Assuming the name of
Friend of the People, he hailed the spirit of Marat with a
courage which only youth could inspire:

Hail! spirit of Marat!   Hail! glorious apostle of Equality!!
Hail! immortal martyr of Liberty!!!   All Hail! thou whose
imperishable title I have assumed; and oh! may the God of
Freedom strengthen me to brave, like thee, the persecution of
tyrants and traitors, or (if so doomed) to meet, like thee, a
martyr's death! [1]

His style, not refined as that of Bronterre nor as florid as
that of O'Connor, was more poignant than that of either of
them.   His exhortation to revolt was direct.   Stephens
suggested that " Englishmen have the right not only to *have*
arms, but *to take them up* in defence of their lives, their
wives and children, for their homes and their hearths." [2]
Harney made it his " arduous task " to urge *war* with
traitors, *" war to the knife."*   In his paper he printed

---

[1] *The London Democrat*, April 13, 1839.
[2] *A Sermon Preached at Primrose Hill, on Sunday, May 12, 1839.*

" Scenes and Sketches from the French Revolution," depict-
ing events and leaders of the movement, " in order that the
present generation may derive a lesson from the deeds of
the past," learn to avoid the errors, and, in the revolution
" which will speedily take place " in England, " imitate the
heroic, God-like deeds of the sons of republican France."
He called upon the poor and oppressed, the young and the
brave, " to strike the home blow, the final blow, the death
blow for old England and Freedom," and assuring them
that no army could withstand a million of armed men, he
exhorted the workingmen to be armed and prepared to
exercise their " first and holiest right—the sacred right
of insurrection ":

Men of the East and West, men of the North and South,
your success lies with yourselves, depend upon yourselves alone,
and your cause will be triumphant . . . Prepare! Prepare!!
Prepare!!! Listen not to the men who would preach delay.
The man who would now procrastinate is a traitor, and may
your vengeance light upon his head. . . . Let me exhort you to
arm. . . . *Arm* to protect your aged parents, *arm* for your
wives and children, *arm* for your sweethearts and sisters,
arm to drive tyranny from the soil and oppression from the
judgment-seat. Your country, your posterity, your God demands of you to *arm!* Arm!! Arm!!! . . . Come, then,
men of the North, from your snow-capped hills; come, then,
men of the South, from your sunlit valleys; come to the gathering; unite, fraternize, arm, and you will be free.[1]

As a speaker, Harney was far below the mark. But he
always had a sufficient stock of " strong words ", which
were in great demand by the masses, and his rôle was more
of an agitator than of a leader.[2]

[1] *The London Democrat*, April 20, 1839.
[2] *Cf.* R. G. Gammage, *History of the Chartist Movement*, Newcastle-
on-Tyne and London, 1894, pp. 29-30.

Henry Vincent, " the English Demosthenes ", was another man who helped blow the embers of popular discontent into a consuming flame of revolt. The son of a
poor silver-smith, he was compelled to earn his livelihood
at the age of eleven. Unable to give him a good education,
his father inculcated in him, however, a love for freedom
and justice. Vincent became interested in politics in 1828,
when he was but fifteen years of age. He was subsequently
an active member of the Political Unions at Hull and London and was one of the members who were deputed by the
London Working Men's Association to agitate for the
Charter. He was a popular orator of great skill and he
used his talents to rouse the passions of the people. Judging by the portrait drawn of him by one of the Chartists,
he was the most graceful and winning orator on the Chartist side:

With a fine mellow flexible voice, a florid complexion, and
excepting in intervals of passion, a most winning expression,
he had only to present himself in order to win all hearts over
to his side. His attitude was perhaps the most easy and
graceful of any popular orator of the time. For fluency of
speech he rivaled all his contemporaries, few of whom were
anxious to stand beside him on the platform. His rare power
of imitation irresistibly drew peals of laughter from the gravest
audience. His versatility, which enabled him to change from
the grave to the gay and *vice versa,* and to assume a dozen
various characters in almost as many minutes, was one of the
secrets of his success. With the fair sex, his slight hand-
some figure, the merry twinkle of his eye, his incomparable
mimicry, his passionate bursts of enthusiasm, the rich music
of his voice, and above all, his appeals for the elevation of
woman, rendered him a universal favorite.[1]

[1] Gammage, *op. cit.,* p. 11.

While the list of the leaders and agitators during the first stages of the movement is by no means complete, special mention must be made of *John Frost*, the " martyr magistrate ", who ventured to carry the propaganda of revolt into practice and who subsequently won the hearts of all liberty-seeking people.

The son of humble parents, Frost was born on the 25th of May, 1786, at Newport. In his boyhood, he displayed great abilities. His early education, however, was quite limited, as he lost his father while he was yet in cradle and was brought up by his grandfather, a boot and shoe maker, who cherished the hope of making his grandson useful in his business. After sending him to school in Bristol for a few years, he indentured John to his business. The boy was released, however, through the interference of an uncle, and, at the age of sixteen, was apprenticed to a tailor. Later he became an assistant to a woolen draper in Bristol. At the age of twenty, he went to London, where he worked at the latter trade. At the solicitations of his mother, he returned to Newport and established himself as a draper and tailor. In 1822 a certain Mr. Protheroe, an influential politician of Newport, sued Frost's uncle for an alleged debt of £150. The suit was decided in favor of Protheroe. As bail for his uncle, Frost threatened to expose Protheroe unless his loss were refunded to him. This threat was construed by the court as an attempt at extortion, and to avoid the payment of £1000 damages awarded against him, Frost sold his whole stock, paid all his creditors, with the exception of one relative who had him arrested for a debt of £200. He then surrendered himself as insolvent. In the meantime, an action for libel was brought against him on the ground that he had alluded to the jury as having been ' packed ' and to the witnesses as perjurers. For this, he paid the penalty of six months' confinement in Goldbath

Fields Prison at London. Popular opinion was, however, in favor of Frost. After his release from prison, he was met on the road, three miles out of Newport, by about fifteen thousand persons with flags and bands of music. He was drawn in the carriage by his townspeople until they reached the bridge, when he was taken out, placed in a chair and carried on men's shoulders in triumph around town.

In his youth, while in London, Frost used to attend meetings of political clubs at which the writings of Thomas Paine and other radicals were discussed. It was then that he became imbued with radical ideas which he cherished all his life. An avowed adherent of Cobbett, he entered the political arena of his native town in 1817. He was an indefatigable advocate of universal suffrage long before the Charter was formulated by the London Working Men's Association. In recognition of his work for municipal reform, he was elected in 1831 to the town council of Newport. In 1836, he was appointed by the Secretary of State to the position of borough magistrate. At the same time he was also a Poor Law Guardian. In 1837, he was elected mayor of Newport. In all these offices, Frost distinguished himself for his ability, efficiency, and justice. As Poor Law Guardian, he exerted all his powers to counteract the cruelties of the law. He joined the Newport Working Men's Association in 1838 and took an active part in the proceedings and plans of the organization. The miners, colliers and iron workers were proud of their friend, the magistrate, and accorded him all the honors of a leader.

In his relations with people, Frost was always liked for his kind disposition, mild manners and benevolence. Yet it was not for these personal attributes that he won the affection of the masses. His Chartist career, however, forming as it does an integral part of the history of the movement, must be deferred to a later chapter.

CHAPTER IX

The people's voice is heard around,
And martyr's blood cries from the ground;
Demanding justice for the brave,
And freedom for the British slave.
On! on ye sons of dear-bought fame,
Your long-lost rights you must regain.
Make tyrants crouch, and traitors see
That Britain's sons shall yet be free.
—William Aitken.

THE PEOPLE

THE first period of the Chartist movement was marked
by a state of ominous excitement in all parts of the country. The agitators for the "six points" joined hands with
the antagonists of the New Poor Law and the factory
system and spread the spirit of discontent, until the response
of the masses was as great as their distress. Within a very
short time after its publication, the People's Charter gained
millions of adherents. The temper of the people could not
be mistaken. Illegal underground societies with sinister
objects sprang up alongside of Chartist organizations. An
authentic description of one of those societies is given by a
contemporary radical who in 1838 was invited to join a
" Foreign Affairs Committee " at Birmingham:

The object of the society I found to be to cut off Lord
Palmerston's head. Things were bad among workmen in
those days, and I had no doubt somebody's head ought to be
cut off, and I hoped they had hit upon the right one. The
secretary was a Chartist leader named Warden, who ended by
cutting his own head off instead, which showed confusion of

ideas by which Lord Palmerston profited. Poor Warden cut
his own throat.[1]

The first important public demonstration in favor of the
Charter was held at Glasgow on the 28th of May, 1838,
under the auspices of the Working Men's Association. In
order to render the demonstration most effective, the Birmingham Political Union sent a fraternal delegation headed
by Thomas Attwood. The procession of about two hundred thousand working men and women was arranged with
great pomp. Forty bands of music were placed at equal
distances, and over two hundred flags and banners with
various devices were carried along the line of the march. The
Birmingham delegates were met with an outburst of enthusiasm and were accorded great honors, in appreciation of the
prestige they lent to the demonstration. Of the speeches,
the most characteristic was that of Thomas Attwood, who
explained the objects of the Charter and developed a plan
of petitioning Parliament. Regarding the movement as
purely political, he warned the people that they had against
them "the whole of the aristocracy, nine-tenths of the gentry, the great body of the clergy, and all the pensioners,
sinecurists, and bloodsuckers that feed on the vitals of the
people." But he spoke in a most hopeful strain of his own
class, declaring that if Parliament refused to concede the
popular demands, the workingmen, together with their
friends of the middle class, should proclaim a "sacred
strike." Attwood's expectations of support from the middle
class was strengthened by the fact that prominent members
of that class participated in the demonstration. The provincial Scotch merchants and manufacturers were not yet

[1] George Jacob Holyoake, *Sixty Years of an Agitator's Life*, London, 1900, vol. ii, p. 77.

conscious of the real causes which spurred the working class to the struggle. Assurances of the peaceful designs of the leaders were also given by a delegate from the London Working Men's Association, and the middle class was fairly represented at the banquet which took place in the evening.

Things did not run so smoothly at the manifestation in Newcastle-on-Tyne which was held by about eighty thousand persons on the 27th of June, 1838, the date of the coronation of Victoria. To begin with, the inscriptions on the banners were not of a conciliatory character. One of them expressed exaltation of "Freedom" in Byron's words:

> When once more her hosts assemble,
> Let the tyrants only tremble;
> Smile they at this idle threat?
> Crimson tears may follow yet.

Another motto, taken from the same poet and characteristic of a number of others, referred to " Revolution ":

> I've seen some nations, like o'er-loaded asses,
> Kick off their burdens, meaning the high classes.

The speeches were delivered in a rather defiant strain. One of the speakers, a working man, declared that the people would use " every means,—not every legal means, mark!— but every means for the attainment of universal suffrage." He adverted to the coronation of the Queen in no conventional style:

They had the representative of the despot Nicholas, and of the sleek tyrant Louis Philippe, and the representatives from all their brother tyrants, assisting to crown sovereign of a great nation a little girl who would be more usefully and properly employed at her needle; but the people would be no longer led away by their gaudy trappings; they would look to themselves and to their families, for if they saw the gewgaws of royalty on the one side, they would see the damnable Bastile on the other.

Feargus O'Connor was one of the star speakers. With his characteristic wit and sarcasm he assailed the New Poor Law:

Harry Brougham said they wished no poor law as every young man ought to lay up provision for old age; yet, while he said this with one side of his mouth, he was screwing the other side to get his retiring pension raised from £4,000 to £5,000 a year. But if the people had their rights they would not pay his salary. Harry would go to the treasury, he would knock, but Cerberus would not open the door, he would say, "Who is there?", and then luckless Harry would answer, "It's an ex-chancellor coming for his £1,250, a quarter's salary"; but Cerberus would say, "There have been a dozen of ye here to-day already, and there is nothing for ye." Then Harry would cry, "Oh! what will become of me! what shall I do!" and Cerberus would say, "Go into the Bastile that you have provided for the people!" Then when Lord Harry and Lady Harry went into the Bastile, the keeper would say, "This is your ward to the right, and this, my lady, is your ward to the left; we are Malthusians here, and are afraid you would breed, therefore you must be kept asunder." If he witnessed such a scene as this he might have some pity for Lady Brougham, but little pity would be due to Lord Harry.[1]

While O'Connor was speaking, a body of dragoons, a line of cavalry and a column of infantry appeared near the meeting. This caused great indignation among the crowd. O'Connor expressed his regret that the men were not in a condition to repel force by force. He warned the " brats of aristocracy " to take care " lest they dared the people to assemble and bring their arms too—they would find there

[1] R. G. Gammage, *op. cit.*, p. 26.

were gallant hearts and virtuous arms under a black coat as well as under a red one." The troops were apparently determined to provoke the people to resistance, but the discretion of the people averted a riot, and the meeting was concluded in perfect order.

Public meetings were also held with distinct success in Sunderland and Northampton. The addresses by Vincent and others were received with great enthusiasm. The Whig rule was contrasted with the honeyed promises made by the party before it came into power. Unanimous resolutions in favor of the People's Charter were carried with shouts of joy and defiance. These meetings were followed on the 6th of August by a great demonstration at Birmingham. Arranged under the auspices of the famous Political Union of that city, the parade attracted the workingmen of the whole manufacturing district. About two hundred thousand persons were said to have participated in the procession. The Birmingham division was followed by six others from Wolverhampton, Walsall, Dudley, Halesowen, Warwick and Studley.

The trades were represented with their flags and banners inscribed with appropriate mottoes. Feargus O'Connor was introduced amidst loud cheers, as representing six towns in Yorkshire. Thomas Attwood, who presided at the meeting, reiterated his moral force policy, but at the same time threatened the House of Commons that should the Charter not be speedily granted, the people would be forced to exercise a little gentle compulsion. He again suggested a *general strike* of one week as a means of impressing the government. It was at this meeting that O'Connor for the first time introduced his physical force notions. The people yearned for a strong word, and he knew how to please them. The whole tenor of his speech was in harmony with the exhortation to " flesh every sword to the hilt." While the crowd demonstrated its approval of O'Connor's sentiments, the local leaders could hardly repress their feelings against the speaker. The meeting, however, was concluded in perfect peace. Important resolutions were adopted calling upon all workingmen to sign a *National Petition* for the enactment of the Charter and to elect delegates to a *General Convention of the Industrious Classes.*[1]

O'Connor's allusion to physical force caused unfavorable comment in the press and great anxiety among the leaders of the London Working Men's Association. As the 17th of September was fixed for a grand demonstration in London, the Association seized the opportunity to repudiate O'Connor by instructing its speakers " to keep as closely as possible to the two great questions of the meeting—*the Charter* and *the Petition*—and as far as possible to avoid all extraneous matter or party politics, as well as every abusive or violent expression which may tend to injure our glorious cause."[2]

Apprehensive of fostering the sentiments created by the Birmingham manifestation, the London Working Men's Association endeavored to have the metropolitan meeting arranged with as little pomp and display as was possible under the circumstances. In order to invest the proceedings with some air of authority, the high bailiff of Westminster was requested to convene the meeting. It may have been due to these circumstances that the Palace Yard demonstration, although represented by delegates from eighty-nine towns, was attended by a comparatively small assembly of about thirty thousand persons. Practically every speaker cautioned against violence. But this very fact betrayed

[1] *Cf. infra*, ch. x.
[2] William Lovett, *op. cit.*, p. 181.

the alarm which was felt by the leaders. It was evident that the mood of the masses was beyond control. One of the speakers, a delegate from Newcastle, referred to the right of the people to assert their own independence in no ambiguous terms:

The men of the north are well organized. The men of New-castle would dare to defend with their arms what they utter with their tongues, as the military would have learned on the coronation day had they made any attack upon the meeting. We are willing to try all moral means that are left, we are willing to try a throne, so long as it is conducive to the happiness of the people; we are willing to have an aristocracy, so long as they behave themselves civilly; but we think we have a right to have a reciprocity of rights, and if not, we are prepared to go against the throne and the aristocracy. The men of the Tyne and the Wear would not draw their swords until their enemies draw upon them, but having once put their hands to the plough they would never look back.[1]

O'Connor, who appeared as a representative of forty or fifty towns in Scotland and England, delivered one of his wittiest speeches. The people, he said, were called pick-pockets. There was, however, a striking difference between a poor pickpocket and a rich pickpocket: "the poor man picked the rich man's pocket to fill his belly, and the rich man picked the poor man's belly to fill his pocket." He proclaimed that the people did not want the obsolete constitution of tallow and wind, but a constitution "of a rail-road genius, propelled by steam power and enlightened by the rays of gas." Every conquest which was called honor-able had been achieved by *physical force*, but the Chartists did not want it, because "if all hands were pulling for universal suffrage, they would soon pull down the stronghold

[1] Gammage, *op. cit.*, p. 49.

of corruption." O'Connor was followed by several speakers who alluded to physical force in similar vein. A delegate from Manchester expressed his conviction that the people had a right to arm in defence of their liberties and, if the Petition failed, he defied " the power of any government or any armed Bourbon police " to put down the armed people.[1]

The meeting which lasted over five hours adopted Lovett's resolution in favor of the People's Charter and responded to the Birmingham call by collecting about sixteen thousand signatures to the National Petition and appointing eight delegates to the General Convention which was to meet in London " to watch over the presentation of the Petition and to obtain, by all legal and constitutional means, the enactment of the People's Charter."

In order to avoid an open rupture with O'Connor and, at the same time, to counteract the effect of the " physical force swagger ", the London Working Men's Association, immediately after the Palace Yard demonstration, prepared an *Address to the Irish People*, imploring " the co-operation of rich and poor, male and female, the sober, the reflecting, and the industrious " to carry forward the principles of moral force:

We are not going to affirm that we have been altogether guiltless of impropriety of language, for when the eye dwells on extremest poverty trampled on by severe oppression, the heart often forces a language from the tongue which sober reflection would redeem, and sound judgment condemn. But we deny that we are influenced by any other feelings than a desire to see our institutions peaceably and orderly based upon principles of justice. We believe that a Parliament composed of the wise and good of all classes, would devise means

[1] Gammage, *op. cit.*, pp. 50-53.

of improving the condition of the millions, without injury to the just interests of the few. We feel that unjust interests have been fostered under an unjust system, that it would be equally unjust to remove without due precaution; and, when due, individual indemnification. We are as desirous as the most scrupulous conservative of protecting all that is good, wise and just in our institutions, and to hold as sacred and secure the domain of the rich equally with the cottage of the poor. But we repeat that we seek to effect our object in peace, with no other force than that of argument or persuasion.[1]

Regardless of the fact that the Address was signed " on behalf of one hundred and thirty-six workingmen's and radical associations ", actual events showed that the influence of the London Working Men's Association was on the wane. The meetings began to assume a formidable aspect even as early as the autumn of 1838. The Manchester demonstration of September 25th was arranged on a gigantic scale. There was scarcely a village in the Lancashire district that did not contribute its quota to the assembly of about three hundred thousand persons who demonstrated their determination to have the Charter become the law of the land. Practically all workshops and factories throughout the district were closed. The hundreds of flags and banners had various devices and mottoes of a threatening character. " Murder demands justice " was the comment inscribed under a picture of the Peterloo massacre. Another banner represented a hand grasping a dagger and bore the gruesome inscription: " Oh, tyrants! will you force us to this?" A spirit of enthusiasm pervaded the line, and the warnings of vengeance brought forth deafening cheers of the crowds. O'Connor and Stephens, who were among the speakers, received a royal reception. The

---

[1] William Lovett, *op. cit.*, pp. 188-9.

meeting which was presided over by John Fielden, the popular advocate of factory reform and opponent of the New Poor Law, adopted a resolution in favor of the Charter and elected eight delegates to the Convention.

The Manchester demonstration was followed on the 15th of October by one in the west of Yorkshire, Peep Green having been selected as the fittest place between Leeds and Huddersfield. The gathering comprised about two hundred and fifty thousand persons, who enjoyed all the attractions of the other manifestations, including bands of music, banners, flags, inscriptions, and addresses by O'Connor and other stars. Similar demonstrations were subsequently held in Liverpool and in a number of other cities all over the country, which adopted resolutions in favor of the People's Charter and elected representatives to the General Convention.

The people of the West were agitated by their favorite orator, Henry Vincent. He kept the workingmen of Bristol, Bath, Bradford, Cheltenham and other cities in a state of constant excitement. A great pet of the women, he organized a number of radical female associations, and hundreds of names were enrolled every day in favor of the Charter. He also succeeded in establishing his supremacy in the Welsh territory. This was a distinct victory for the young and ardent orator. On account of the relatively high wages paid to the operatives in the coal and iron districts, the Welsh workingmen had been considered immune from all radicalism. Vincent, however, roused the dormant discontent of the wage-earners and within a short time, in spite of the urgent appeals made by high personages against the Charter, gained the unflinching support of the masses and actually prepared them for the " death-dance of revolution."

The frequent manifestations in favor of the Charter

fostered the spirit of revolt. The *six points* were represented as tantamount to the sum total of human happiness, and the working people decided to win the Charter at all hazards. As the demonstrations by day incurred loss of time during working hours and as the authorities started to thwart indoor meetings by refusing the use of the commodious town halls, the leaders seized the opportunity of fanning the passions of the people by arranging a series of torch-light processions in a number of cities, including the industrial centres of Bolton, Ashton, Stockport, Staleybridge, Hyde and Leigh. The meetings proved a great success, attracting in each case tens of thousands of working men and women who pledged their lives in allegiance to the cause. The processions usually passed the principal streets of each city cheering the leaders and denouncing those newspapers, magistrates and manufacturers who had shown antagonism to the movement. Bands of music preceeded the march, while banners of various sizes and colors and bearing revolutionary devices were carried in the blazing stream of torch lights. " For children and wife, we'll war to the knife! "; " He that hath no sword, let him sell his garment and buy one "; " Remember the bloody deeds of Peterloo ", and " Tyrants, believe and tremble ",—these were common mottoes at the demonstrations. The meetings were always attended by one or more of the *lions of the movement*,—O'Connor, Stephens, and Harney being the chief speakers. At the torch-light meeting which was held on the 14th of November, 1838, at Hyde, Stephens, surrounded by a large number of men wearing and carrying upon poles *red caps of liberty*, branded the manufacturers as a gang of murderers whose blood was required to satisfy the demands of public justice. He advised every one of his hearers to get a large carving knife which might be used to cut either a rasher of bacon or the men who opposed their demands.

The agitators of physical force found the field ready.   As a matter of fact, thousands of men in all parts of the country were at that time secretly making arms.   The Manchester delegate to the Palace Yard demonstration in London declared that the people of Lancashire were armed, that he himself had seen the arms hanging over the mantlepieces of the poor.[1]   At the torch-light meetings, weapons were brandished and frequent discharges from firearms were made for no other purpose than to impress the authorities with the fact that the people were armed.   At the Hyde meeting Stephens asked his hearers if they were ready to resist force by force.   The loud firing of arms and the forest of hands raised in response to his question satisfied the agitator that it was *all right*, that the people knew how to repel the enemy in a way which would tell sharper tales than their tongues.[2]

The excitement grew even more intense after the publication of a letter which Lord John Russell sent on the 22nd of November, 1838, to the Lancashire magistrates, requesting them to announce the illegality of torchlight meetings and to use all means to prevent and disperse such gatherings.   Lord Russell was denounced as the tool of the middle class particularly because only a few weeks before he had given expression to sentiments of a diametrically opposite nature.   Speaking at a dinner given in his honor by the civic authorities of Liverpool and referring to the public demonstrations in favor of the Charter, he said:

There were some, perhaps, who would put down such meetings; but such was not his opinion nor that of the Government with which he acted.   He thought the people had a right to meet.   If they had no grievances, common sense would

[1] Gammage, *op. cit.*, p. 52.
[2] *Ibid.*, p. 97.

speedily come to the rescue and put an end to those meetings. It was not from free discussion, it was not from the unchecked declaration of public opinion that government had anything to fear. There was fear when men were driven by force to secret combinations. There was the fear, there was the danger, and not in free discussion.[1]

The people, in their indignation, defied the government and publicly trampled under foot the royal proclamation of the middle of December which, on penalty of imprisonment, enjoined all persons to desist from participating in torch-light meetings. The chasm between the workingmen and the middle class became ever wider. If a workingman failed to abuse the middle class, he was himself vilified and denounced. The bearing of arms became more general. Holyoake witnessed in Birmingham that those who had no better weapons " sharpened an old file and stuck it in a haft." [2]   The *Dundee Advertiser* of April 12, 1839, declared that " a number of infatuated individuals " had commenced drilling and intimated that the authorities were keeping an eye over them: " Shackles in place of pikes will shortly be the upshot to those who engage in such dangerous pastime." Even women started to organize themselves and in several instances procured arms.[3] This was particularly striking in Welsh towns where Vincent had perfect control over the situation and where he had organized a number of female Chartist associations. At a public meeting in Pentonville he invoked the people to swear that they would be ready to act if their demands were rejected by the government, and he called upon all who were prepared to turn out to hold up their arms. His appeal was answered

---

[1] *Cf.* Hansard, *op. cit.*, vol. xlix, 1839, p. 455.

[2] Holyoake, *op. cit.*, vol. i, p. 83.

[3] *Cf.* Richard Marsden in *The London Democrat*, May 11, 1839.

by thunderous shouts, "We swear! We swear!" and a majority of those present readily raised their arms.[1]

The arrest of Stephens, the first Chartist victim, for attending illegal meetings and using violent language, increased the excitement to an alarming extent. The masses were not satisfied with the mere possession of arms and sought practical advice on military operations. The widely circulated *Defensive Instructions to the People* by Colonel Macerone was supplemented by special articles on *Military Science* by Major Beniowski in *The London Democrat*. Extolling the " science of killing " as the most useful and the most sublime of all sciences, small bands of men were instructed how to resist the attacks of a more numerous enemy and how to render offensive operations most advantageous for strategical and tactical purposes.[2]

The military science is, simply, that which teaches you how to maim and kill as many of your enemies as possible, and also how to protect yourselves against a similar propensity of your opponents. If those who first reduced this " glorious " wholesale murder to rules had no end in view but to gratify the beastly passions of the *few*, they were abominable monsters, whom it would have been the duty of every honest man to smother at their birth. But if their intention was the defence of the enslaved, oppressed, and starving *millions*, to curb ambition or to oppose the claims of incomprehensible rights, mankind ought to erect altars to their memory. In this last case, the science of killing and destroying is the most

---

[1] *The Chartist Riots at Newport*, November, 1839, 2d ed., Newport, 1881, p. 15.

[2] The attitude of the Chartists towards war and armaments was practically identical both in spirit and expression with the *ante bellum* professions of the modern socialists. In view of the general interest in the present war, it was considered not amiss to reprint a characteristic dialogue between a *moral force* Whig and a Chartist, giving the " school-master's " view of the subject. See Appendix D.

useful and necessary of all the sciences; it is, in fact, the only one which, if universally known by the people at large, could prevent homicide at all. Unhappily this terribly sublime knowledge is not to be attained without difficulty. . . . It is only by a continual, active, and concentrated application of an undivided mind, prompted by a peculiar natural disposition, or inflamed by extraordinary events, that any man can attain it.[1]

The *extraordinary events* were in the process of realization. The talk of preparedness and resistance impelled the *physical force* advocates to attempt a wide agitation among the soldiers. The Chartists were urged to impart all information about the movement to the men in the barracks and were assured that the soldiers were "on the right scent", that they read O'Connor's *Northern Star* and that even the *London Democrat* "found its way into the army". Discussing the question as to what the soldiers would do in the coming struggle, a correspondent of the *physical force* weekly [2] expressed his belief, which was based on personal observations, that they would not defend "the citadel of corruption" by cutting the throats of their fathers, their brothers, their mothers, their sisters and sweethearts, but, on the contrary, would "supply the places of the moral-force men" who would turn traitors to the cause. Whether or not the people shared this belief, the "extraordinary events" ran into a different channel.

[1] *The London Democrat*, April 27, 1839.
[2] *Ibid.*, May 4, 1839.

CHAPTER X

THE PETITION, THE CONVENTION AND THE GOVERNMENT

THE idea of a National Petition, as well as the plan of a General Convention of the Industrious Classes, originated with the Birmingham Political Union. Nothing can be farther from the truth than the "historical" assertion that the Petition and the Convention were undertaken in simulation of the tactics of the French Revolutionists. Both proposals emanated from the *moral force* group at the Birmingham demonstration of August 6, 1838, but once adopted they were made most use of by the preachers of revolt.

The National Petition is credited to the pen of R. K. Douglas, the editor of the *Birmingham Journal*. It demands the enactment of but five points—that of *equal representation* having been omitted probably because it was confounded with *universal suffrage*. The petition is couched in terms far from revolutionary. It is lacking not only in vigor of expression, but also in definiteness of aim. The author apparently took extreme caution not to offend any class or any group of individuals. The influence of Thomas Attwood is seen throughout the petition, particularly in the demand to abolish "the laws which make food dear, and those which, by making money scarce, make labor cheap". Not a word is said about the New Poor Law or about factory legislation; not a hint is given of the unjust distribution of wealth. On the contrary, repeated references are made to the burden imposed on the capitalist class, and the House is told " that the capital of the master must no longer be deprived of its due reward ".[1] The petition complains against the load of taxes which affects capital as well as labor, and alludes to other matters which, in previous petitions, were labeled by Bronterre as " unconsequential rubbish ".[2] It would have been amazing to see the working class agitated by the Petition, had that agitation not been the expression of a much deeper cause. It was the idea of the Petition and not its contents that contained the promise of the holy land and that animated the people. It is on this account that the National Petition must be considered one of the most remarkable documents in the history of the English labor movement. The call for a national subscription for the petition received a generous response. Men and women devoted night after night to the collection of funds and signatures and submitted good-humoredly to every sort of reply to their solicitations. The contributions were necessary in order to defray the cost of the campaign and to support the members of the Convention.

The opening of the General Convention of the Industrious Classes took place on the 4th of February, 1839, at the British Coffee House, Cockspur Street, London. The subsequent sessions were held at the Hall of the Dr. Johnson Tavern, Fleet Street. Of the fifty-three delegates representing various cities from all parts of the kingdom, three were magistrates, six newspaper editors, two clergymen, two physicians, while the others were shopkeepers, tradesmen and laborers. The objects of the General Convention were declared to be as follows:

1. To collect the signatures already appended to the *National*

[1] See Appendix C.
[2] *Cf. supra*, p. 82.

Petition in different parts of the Kingdom, and to use every possible exertion to cause it to be signed by every reformer in these realms.

2. To use the most efficient means and choose the most fitting time for introducing the *National Petition* into the Commons' House of Parliament.

3. To select such members of Parliament as the majority of the delegates may deem proper, for introducing the bill entitled the *People's Charter* into both Houses of Parliament and enforcing its adoption.

4. To wait upon the members of the House of Commons (and, if necessary, upon Her Majesty and the Peers of these realms) and individually and collectively enforce upon them the claims of the industrious millions to their just share of political power and the necessity and justice for complying with their demands by supporting the *National Petition* and voting for the *People's Charter*.

5. To create and extend, by every constitutional means, an enlightened and powerful public opinion in favor of the above objects, and justly and righteously impress that opinion upon the legislature, as the best means of securing the prosperity and happiness of our country and averting those calamities which exclusive legislation and corrupt government will necessarily produce.

Notwithstanding this peaceful declaration, the delegates repeatedly proclaimed the Convention the only representative and legally elected body, assumed functions of a legislative body, and adopted a set of rules and regulations, including those relating to future elections of delegates and the duties of the constituencies. The presentation of the National Petition was postponed until the 6th of May, in order to procure a larger number of signatures. Missionaries were sent out to various towns to agitate for the Charter and to collect signatures to the Petition. In the interim, the delegates in London busied themselves with a variety of problems. The "grievances of Ireland", "the suffering in the manufacturing districts", "the factory system", "the New Rural Police Bill", were but a few of the subjects that gave rise to long and heated discussions. "In fact," Lovett confesses, "the love of talk was as characteristic of our little house as the big one at Westminster." [1] Of more immediate interest was the question of "*ulterior measures*" to be adopted if the petition were rejected on the 6th of May. Care was taken that the discussions and proceedings of the Convention be reported in a way to excite the passions of the masses. The addresses of the delegates dwelling at length on the distress and misery of the people were printed and distributed broadcast among the industrial and agricultural wage-earners. The speech of delegate Richard Marsden of Preston attracted particular attention because it was not an elaborated statement of a social investigator or an embellished picture of a professional agitator. It was the cry of actual despair that pierced the hearts of all who heard or read his narrative. As an illustration of the effects of the factory system, Marsden presented the case of his own wife and children who were entirely destitute of the bare necessities of life. With an infant at her breast, his wife was so emaciated in consequence of lack of nourishment that when the baby tried to nurse, it drew the mother's blood. [2]

The division in the ranks of the Chartist delegates was evident from the beginning. The first collision between the moral force adherents and the followers of the Marat policy took place at the very opening of the Convention. At the first few sessions the London Working Men's Association had the upper hand. Lovett was elected secretary in

[1] Lovett, *op. cit.*, p. 204.

[2] This statement was subsequently confirmed to Gammage by Mrs. Marsden. See Gammage, *op. cit.*, p. 108.

spite of the strong opposition on the part of the physical force advocates. The missionaries who were sent out of the Metropolis to obtain signatures to the National Petition were instructed " to refrain from all violent and unconstitutional language and not to infringe the law in any manner by word or deed." The spirit of enthusiasm that pervaded the Convention did not last long, however. Some delegates soon tired of formal speeches and grew impatient with the counselors of a policy of peaceful waiting. In allegiance to the London Democratic Association, they created discord within and without the Convention assembly. Harney was most emphatic in his condemnation of the cowardice and imbecility of the Convention and urged the people to prepare for the approaching struggle. At Smithfield he appeared at an open-air meeting wearing a red cap of liberty in imitation of the French Revolutionists. The London Democratic Association, of which he was secretary, adopted three resolutions :

1. That if the Convention did its duty, the Charter would be the law of the land in less than a month.
2. That no delay should take place in the presentation of the National Petition.
3. That every act of injustice and oppression should be immediately met by resistance.

These resolutions were submitted to the Convention on the 4th of March and caused several motions to be made condemnatory of the conduct of the extreme Chartists. One delegate censured Harney for making use of French revolutionary expressions and French emblems. Another demanded an apology from Harney and his followers, on penalty of expulsion, for addressing the resolutions to the Convention. Even Bronterre recorded his opinion that the Convention must be on guard not to prejudice the government against the Petition, while Lovett's close friends, Hetherington, Cleave, and others, protested against the use of all emblems which might compromise the Convention and thus injure the cause. In the language of Lovett, Harney and two other delegates "deemed it advisable to make the apology required."[1] It was, however, after a lapse of but a few days that the censured agitators succeeded in establishing their supremacy. On the 11th of March, 1839, Harney, O'Connor, Frost, Bronterre, and others addressed a crowded meeting which was called under the auspices of the Convention, at the Crown and Anchor, and at which they publicly attacked the inactivity of the Convention and exhorted the Chartists to arm themselves for the approaching crisis. Bronterre declared that the only reason he did not advise the people to arm themselves was because the law did not let him. He was only a historian, he said, and merely reported the "fact" that all the people of Leeds and of Lancashire *had* procured arms. While he could not urge his hearers to do likewise, he was certain that the Petition would be helped along, if all the people of England followed the example of his friends in the North. He accordingly appealed to them to organize, to put themselves in such a position of defense that if an attempt were made to suspend the laws and the constitution of the country, they should be able to send the traitors to eternity. The enthusiastic cheers of the audience at every allusion to physical force left no doubt that the metropolitan workingmen endorsed the sentiments of the speakers.

The speeches stirred up a great deal of hostile criticism in the press which provoked three Birmingham delegates to tender their resignations "because the Convention was

[1] Lovett, *op. cit.*, p. 204.

not guided by principles of peace, law and order." This
act on the part of the moral force delegates branded them
in the eyes of the people as traitors and gave a new impetus
to the physical force agitation. It was then that the *London Democrat* was established to launch a systematic campaign for *preparedness* and to preach *insurrection* as the
only means for the people to obtain the Charter. All legal
and constitutional efforts inspired little hope for the immediate success of the National Petition, and the workingmen
were urged to lose no time in organizing and preparing
themselves for the coming struggle, "such as the world
has not yet witnessed." The Chartists were advised to
inscribe on their banners the mottoes: "Liberty or death",
"the People's Charter and no further delay", "the People's Charter—peaceably if we can, forcibly if we must",
and the people were reminded that their *tyrants* would
never concede justice till they were compelled, till they were
overcome *by fire and sword* and exterminated from the face
of the earth.

The Chartists foresaw the possibility of a prorogation
of Parliament before the presentation of the Petition on
the 6th of May, or before the House could be tested
respecting the Charter. In case of such a contingency,
Harney supported Bronterre's recommendation that, on
the day appointed by the Queen's proclamation for a new
election, the people of each county, city and borough
should assemble at the proper places and nominate men
pledged to the Charter. He was certain that the universal
suffrage candidates would be elected in nineteen out of
every twenty cases. He realized that the election of representatives without enabling them to take their seats in the
House of Commons would present "the veriest farce imaginable". It was, therefore, necessary that each elected

representative should be furnished with a bodyguard of
sturdy *sans-culottes*:

By the time the whole of the representatives arrived in the
environs of the metropolis, they would have with them not
less than a *million of men*. This would soon settle the matter.
"The million of men," with their representatives, would en-
camp for one night on Hampstead-heath, and the following
morning march upon London, where myriads would hail with
songs of joy their march through Parliament, *safely* conducting their representatives past the Horse-guards, should the
shopocratic-elected scoundrels be fools enough to have previously seated themselves in the tax-trap. The voice of the
people crying, "Make way for better men," would scatter
them like chaff before the wind; or, should they hesitate to
fly, the job will soon be settled by their being tied neck and
heels and flung into the Thames. As to resistance on the part
of the soldiery, the idea is not to be entertained. What army
could withstand *a million of armed men?* For, of course,
every man would come prepared for the worst; and even
should the tyrants be mad enough to provoke a conflict, can
the result be doubtful? No; within a week not a despot's
breath would pollute the air of England.[1]

The missionaries did not carry out the instructions of
the Convention to refrain from all violent language. Vincent especially exhorted the people to be prepared to resist
the government. At several meetings in Welsh towns, he
called upon the working class to be ready to act after the
6th of May, and that every hill and valley should be prepared to send forth its army, if required by the Convention. At Newport he concluded his speech with the invo-
cation: "To your tents, O Israel! and then with one voice,
one heart, and one blow, perish the privileged orders!
Death to the aristocracy!" In Pentonville he attacked the

[1] *The London Democrat*, April 27, 1839.

government as an atrocious and cannibal system: it doomed
men, women and children to toil in factories from morning
till night in a state approaching starvation, for the purpose
of increasing the wealth of the aristocracy.[1]

Far from rebuking its missionaries, the Convention
acted in harmony with the prevailing spirit of the masses
and, after a long discussion, adopted a resolution to the
effect " that it was admitted by the highest authorities, beyond the possibility of doubt, that the people had the right
to use arms."[2]

In the meantime the government kept a vigilant eye on
the movements of the members of the Convention and the
active Chartists.   Venomous newspaper reports of the
Chartist meetings provoked the government to introduce a
wide system of espionage.   The spies simulated great devotion to the cause and instigated the masses to " speak
out " and to " prove to the government that the people were
in earnest."   Zealous to produce proof to the government
of their usefulness and of their alertness to " discover "
all Chartist plots, they adopted a favorite scheme of teaching the credulous workingmen how to destroy property
and strike terror into the hearts of the " despots ".   One
of these *provocateurs*, Holyoake writes, produced an
explosive liquid which, he said, could be poured into the
sewers and, when ignited, would blow up the whole city of
London.   " This satanic preparation was tried in a cellar
in Judd Street, while I was taking tea in the back parlor
above.   I did not know at the time of the operation going
on below, or it might have interfered with my satisfaction
in the repast on which I was engaged."[3]

[1] *Cf. The Chartist Riots at Newport*, 2nd ed., Newport, 1889, pp. 15-
16; also *The Rise and Fall of Chartism in Monmouthshire*, London,
1840, p. 25.

[2] Lovett, *op. cit.*, p. 205.

[3] Holyoake, *op. cit.*, vol. ii, p. 4.

The activities of magistrate John Frost, the Welsh delegate to the Convention, caused much public discussion, and Lord John Russell was taunted from many quarters for the appointment he had made. Russell then sent Frost a letter inquiring whether he was a delegate to the Convention, as well as whether he had attended a public meeting at Pontypool, at which inflammatory language was used, and notifying him that such actions, if true, must cause his name to be erased from the Commission of the Peace for the county of Monmouth. The answer which Frost sent to Russell gained him unanimous praise from his colleagues who paid him due tribute at a dinner given in his honor in London. His letter, dated at Newport, January 19, 1839, contained a spirited rebuke of the Secretary of State. Its haughty defiance was characteristic of the
· period of unrest. He writes:[1]

In your Lordship's letter of the 16th, there is a mistake. I am not a magistrate for the county of Monmouth, but for the borough of Newport, in the county of Monmouth. In the spring of 1835 the council of the borough recommended me as a proper person to be a justice of the peace. I was appointed, and I believe that the inhabitants will bear honorable testimony as to the manner in which I have performed the duties of that office. Whether your Lordship will retain my name, or cause it to be erased, is to me a matter of perfect indifference, for I set no value on an office dependant for its continuance, not according to the mode in which its duties are performed, but on the will of a Secretary of State.

For what does your Lordship think it incumbent to get my name erased from the commission of the peace? For attending a meeting at Pontypool, on the 1st of January? If the public papers can be credited, your Lordship declared that

[1] See *Rise and Fall of Chartism in Monmouthshire*, London, 1840, pp. 11-13.

such meetings were not only legal but commendable. But "violent and inflammatory language was used at that meeting." . . . There was a time when the Whig Ministry was not so fastidious as to violent and inflammatory language uttered at public meetings.

By what authority does your Lordship assume a power over conduct of mine unconnected with my office? By what authority does your Lordship assign any action of mine, as a private individual, as a justification for erasing my name from the commission of the peace? Am I to hold no opinion of my own, in respect to public matters? Am I to be prohibited from expressing that opinion, if it be unpleasing to Lord J. Russell? If, in expressing that opinion, I act in strict conformity to the law, can it be an offence? If I transgress, is not the law sufficiently stringent to punish me? It appears from the letter of your Lordship that I, if present at a public meeting, should be answerable for language uttered by others. If these are to be the terms on which Her Majesty's commission of the peace are to be holden, take it back again, for surely none but the most servile of men would hold it on such terms.

Is it an offence to be appointed a delegate to convey to the constituted authorities the petitions of the people? . . . I was appointed a justice of the peace to administer the laws within the borough of Newport. Was the appointment made, that the inhabitants might benefit by the proper exercise of the authority intrusted to me? Or was it made to be recalled at the will of your Lordship, although the inhabitants might be perfectly satisfied with the performance of the duty? Your Lordship receives a very large sum of money for holding the office of Secretary of State, paid, in part, out of the taxes raised on the inhabitants of the borough. Does your Lordship owe them no duty? For what is your Lordship invested with authority? To be exercised merely at the caprice of your Lordship, regardless of the effects that may follow? I have served the inhabitants for three years, zealously and gratuitously, and the opinions which I have formed as to the exercise of public authority, teach me that they, and not your

Lordship, ought to decide whether I ought to be struck off the commission of peace.

Filling an humble situation in life, I would yield neither to your Lordship, nor any of your order, in a desire to see my country powerful and prosperous. Twenty years' reading and experience have convinced me that the only method to produce and secure that state of things is a restoration of the ancient constitution. Deeply impressed with this conviction, I have labored to obtain the end, by means recognized by the laws of my country—petition; and for this your Lordship thinks I ought to be stricken off the commission of the peace! Violent and inflammatory language indeed! I am convinced that in my own neighborhood, my attending at public meetings has tended to restrain violent language. . . .

Probably your Lordship is unaccustomed to language of this description; that, my Lord, is a misfortune. Much of evils of life proceed from the want of sincerity in those who hold converse with men in authority. Simple men like those best who prophesy smooth things. . . .

The Chartists rejoiced at the humiliation which Lord Russell received at the hands of one of their leaders. For several months they had brooded over their resentment against the Secretary of State, not so much on account of his suppression of torch-light meetings as on account of his offer of arms to any association of the middle class that would be formed ostensibly for the protection of life and property, but in reality for putting down Chartist assemblies. The policy of Russell, however, was rather vacillating. The meeting of March 11th at the Crown and Anchor, at which Frost was in the chair, was the landmark for both the terrorists and the government. The systematic campaign of the press against the principles of the Charter as tending to robbery and destruction of society was turned with effective force against the representatives of the government who were charged with being, in their cowardice, abettors of sedition. This made Lord Russell cast aside the painful attitude of strained indulgence, on the one hand, and masqued oppression, on the other. A state of open hostility now established itself between the government and the Chartists. The authorities left no doubt as to their determination to handle the situation in a disciplinary way. Russell's order, about the end of March, to strike the name of Frost from the Commission of Peace for attending Chartist meetings, was followed, in April, by the indictment of Stephens and the declaration that the Convention was an *illegal* body, and, in May, by the arrest in London of Vincent who was conveyed to Newport and, together with several other Chartists, committed to Monmouth gaol. The Mayor of Newport had collected evidence against the young orator and his followers in the hope that, if a conviction took place, Chartism in Monmouthshire " would be reckoned among the things that were." [1] The strength of the movement was, however, greatly underestimated. Far from being dismayed, the Chartists challenged their adversaries on more than one occasion.

On the 6th of May, 1839, the National Petition, containing about one million two hundred and eighty-three thousand signatures, was taken to the residence of Thomas Attwood, who had promised to present it to Parliament. By that time, however, Attwood's allegiance to the Chartist cause underwent a marked change. It may have been due to the aggressive policy of the Convention or to the fact that at all times the issue of paper money was more important to him than the People's Charter. Be it as it may, he gave little encouragement to the delegation, expressing his doubt whether, on account of the expected

---

[1] *Cf. Rise and Fall of Chartism in Monmouthshire*, 1840, p. 18.

resignation of Lord Russell from the ministry, he would be able to present the Petition in the near future and refusing to move for leave to bring in a bill entitled the *People's Charter.*

This circumstance, as well as the enmity of the government, made the leaders realize that the Charter would not "be the law of the land in less than a month." The Convention carried O'Connor's motion to adjourn to Birmingham, where the surroundings were thought more favorable because of the general excitement which prevailed both on account of the conduct of the local authorities in suppressing public meetings and of Lord Russell's letter to the magistrates offering arms to the middle class. On the 13th of May the Convention was welcomed in that city by a vast assemblage and resumed its sessions in a buoyant spirit. On the following day, after some discussion, the *Manifesto of the General Convention of the Industrious Classes* was adopted, and ten thousand copies were ordered to be printed for circulation.

The language and the object of the *Manifesto* render it the most remarkable Chartist document. There is no sign of the previous overtures to the middle class, and due respect is paid to the "menaces of employers" and the "power of wealth". The distinct class interests of the working men and women are put in the foreground. Beginning with the declaration that "the government of England is a despotism and her industrious millions slaves"; that her forms of "justice" are subterfuges for legal plunder and class domination; that the "right of the subject" is slavery, without the slave's privilege, and that the Whigs and the Tories are united in their despotic determination to maintain their power and supremacy at any risk, the *Manifesto* continues:

Men and women of Britain, will you tamely submit to the insult? Will you submit to the incessant toil from birth to death, to give in tax and plunder out of every *twelve* hours' labor the proceeds of *nine* hours to support your idle and insolent oppressors? Will you much longer submit to see the greatest blessings of mechanical art converted into the greatest curses of social life?—to see children forced to compete with their parents, wives with their husbands, and the whole of society morally and physically degraded to support the aristocracies of wealth and title? Will you allow your wives and daughters to be degraded; your children to be nursed in misery, stultified by toil, and to become the victims of the vice our corrupt institutions have engendered? Will you permit the stroke of affliction, the misfortunes of poverty, and the infirmities of age to be branded and punished as crimes, and give our selfish oppressors an excuse for rending asunder man and wife, parent and child, and continue passive observers till you and yours become the victims?

Perish the cowardly feeling; and infamous be the passive being who can witness his country's degradation, without a struggle to prevent or a determination to remove it! Rather, like Sampson, would we cling to the pillars which sustain our social fabric, and, failing to base it upon principles of justice, fall victims beneath its ruins. Shall it be said, fellow-countrymen, that four millions of men, capable of bearing arms and defending their country against every foreign assailant, allowed a few domestic oppressors to enslave and degrade them? That they suffered the constitutional right of possessing arms, to defend the constitutional privileges their ancestors bequeathed to them, to be disregarded or forgotten till one after another they have been robbed of their rights, and have submitted to be awed into silence by the bludgeons of policemen? . . .

Men of England, Scotland, and Wales, we have sworn with your aid to achieve our liberties or die! And in this resolve we seek to save our country from a fate we do not desire to witness. If you longer continue passive slaves, the fate of unhappy Ireland will soon be yours, and that of Ireland more

degraded still.   For, be assured, the joyful hope of freedom
which now inspires the millions, if not speedily realized, will
turn into wild revenge.   The sickening thought of unrequited
toil—their cheerless homes—their stunted, starving offspring—
the pallid partners of their wretchedness — their aged parents
pining apart in a workhouse—the state of trade presenting to
their imaginations no brighter prospect—these, together with
the petty tyranny that daily torments them, will exasperate
them to destroy what they are denied the enjoyment of. . . .

Both Whigs and Tories are seeking, by every means in their
power, to crush our peaceful organization in favor of our
Charter.   They are sending their miscreant spies to urge the
people into madness; they are arming the rich against the
poor, and against his fellow-man. . . . We trust, brethren,
that you will disappoint their malignity, and live to regain our
rights by other means,—at least, we trust you will not *commence* the conflict.   We have resolved to obtain our rights,
" peaceably if we may, forcibly if we must "; but woe to those
who begin the warfare with the millions, or who forcibly restrain their peaceful agitation for justice—at one signal they
will be enlightened to their error, and in one brief contest their
power will be destroyed. . . .

The Chartists were called upon to organize *simultaneous*
public meetings for the purpose of petitioning the Queen
" to call good men to her councils ", and, in order to ascertain " the opinions and determination of the people in the
shortest possible time ", a series of questions, or " ulterior
measures ", was to be submitted at each meeting.   Reminding the Chartists that the motto of the Convention was
Union, Prudence and Energy, and assuring them that after
ascertaining the expression of organized public opinion
that body will immediately proceed to carry the will of the
people into execution, the time for the *simultaneous* meetings was limited to the 1st of July.

The " ulterior measures " proposed by the *Manifesto* and

subsequently submitted to the consideration of the *simul-taneous* assemblies were as follows:

1. Whether they will be prepared, at the request of the Convention, to withdraw all sums of money they may individually or collectively have placed in savings' banks, private banks, or in the hands of any person hostile to their just rights?

2. Whether, at the same request, they will be prepared immediately to convert all their paper money into gold and silver?

3. Whether, *if the Convention shall determine that a sacred month will be necessary* to prepare the millions to secure the charter of their political salvation, they will firmly resolve to abstain from their labors during that period, as well as from the use of all *intoxicating drinks?*

4. Whether, according to their old constitutional right—a right which modern legislation would fain annihilate — they have prepared themselves *with the arms of freemen to defend the laws and constitutional privileges their ancestors bequeathed to them?*

5. Whether they will provide themselves with *Chartist candidates*, so as to be prepared to propose them for their representatives at the next general election; and if returned *by show of hands* such candidates to consider themselves veritable representatives of the people—to meet in London at a time hereafter to be determined on?

6. Whether they will resolve *to deal exclusively with Chartists*, and in all cases of persecution rally around and protect all those who may suffer in their righteous cause?

7. Whether by all and every means in their power they will perseveringly contend for the great objects of the People's Charter, and resolve that no counter agitation for a less measure of justice shall divert them from their righteous object?

8. Whether the people will determine to obey all the just and constitutional requests of the majority of the Convention?

The "ulterior measures" did not satisfy all the members of the Convention. They were concocted as a compro-

mise program by the various factions.   One can easily discern the influence of Attwood's followers in the first three
" measures ".   The abstinence proposal was denounced by
Harney and his friends as savoring of humbug, believing
as they did that nothing but the extremest measures would
be of any value.   The radicals carried their recommenda-
tions to ascertain whether the people were ready to resist
the authorities and to take matters in their hands, to elect
and seat their own candidates,[1] to boycott opponents by
dealing *exclusively* with Chartists, and to protect all who
may suffer in the cause.   Lovett, who, as secretary of the
Convention, signed the *Manifesto*,[2] confesses that he " did
an act of folly in being a party to *some of its provisions* ",
but extenuates this " folly ", as it was committed for the
sake of union and for the love and hope he had in the
cause.[3]

While the   *Manifesto* counseled not to " *commence the
conflict* ", the *London Democrat* was untiring in its campaign for insurrection as a " *primary measure* ".   Terror
was advocated as the only means by which the " aristocratic
and shopocratic factions " could be induced to do justice to
the people.   The idea of a " bloodless triumph " was dispensed with as mere " chatter and nonsense ", as the " vengeance of blood is the only means of striking terror to the
hearts of tyrants, especially the relentless tyrants of England—the callous-hearted money-mongers."

It won't be the *organized* masses that will carry the victory.
Oh, no!   *That* depends upon the poor, outcast, friendless
beings who have no home to go to, no food to satisfy the

---

[1] *Cf. supra*, p. 159.

[2] The *Manifesto* was signed on behalf of the Convention by Hugh
Craig, Chairman, and William Lovett, Secretary.

[3] *Cf.* Lovett, *op. cit.*, pp. 208-9.

cravings of hunger, no covering to keep them warm, or even to make them look *decent*, no wherewithal to render their lives worth preserving. The battle . . . will be fought and won by those whom poverty and degradation have rendered outcasts from society—by those who *hide* themselves from the gaze of the world, through the cruel operation of unjust and partially-executed laws. The battle will be fought and won by the *brigands*, as they are called. As for premature outbreaks, indeed, a great deal of stuff and nonsense has been rung in the ears of the people concerning popular commotions. Is the present movement *a real one?* If it is, then too many outbreaks cannot take place. Premature outbreaks, as they are called, are only fatal to sham movements; but, at a time like this, the more the better. . . . What are outbreaks? Are they not ebullitions of popular feeling? Then if numerous outbreaks take place, does it not prove that the *people* are ready? Then, hurrah for a leader! Hurrah for the man who has the energy and courage to unfurl the banner of freedom and lead the people on to victory or death. . . . Government looks upon all parties in the Chartist ranks alike. Neither party can find favor in the eyes of exclusive legislators. Sham radicals, timid radicals, trading radicals, as well as honest and determined democrats, will all alike be persecuted and crushed if "*the step*" be not now taken — if the blow be not now struck. . . . We are all embarked in the same vessel, and a shipwreck would be as fatal to the one party as the other. Let honest men then unite, and the victory is safe, sure and speedy.[1]

The relations of mutual distrust between the government and the Chartists became ever more pronounced. Alarmed at the enthusiastic reception which the Birmingham people accorded the Convention, the government complied with the request of the local authorities and sent a number of

---

[1] *The London Democrat*, May 18, 1839. *Cf.* also issues of May 25, *et seq.*

the London police force to that city. This, in its turn, created ill-feeling in the assembly, and it was due primarily to the timely warnings of O'Connor and Bronterre not to carry arms to the meetings that the "People's Parliament" was saved from police intervention.

On the 17th of May the Convention adjourned to the 1st of July after having passed Bronterre's resolutions: 1st, That peace, law, and order shall continue to be the motto of the Convention, so long as the "oppressors" will act in the same spirit towards the people; otherwise, it shall be deemed a sacred duty of the people "to meet force with force and repel assassination by justifiable homicide"; 2nd, That the Chartists who may attend the *simultaneous* meetings shall avoid carrying offensive weapons about their persons and treat as enemies of the cause any person who may exhibit such weapons, or who "by any other act of folly or wickedness, should provoke a breach of the peace"; 3rd, That the officers who may have charge of the arrangements for the *simultaneous* meetings shall in all cases consult with the local authorities; and 4th, That should the authorities be instigated by the "oppressors in the upper and middle ranks" to assail the people with armed force, the "oppressors" would be held responsible, "in person and property, for any detriment that may result to the people from such atrocious instigation".

The *simultaneous* meetings were held in a great number of cities, towns, and villages with distinct success. Conservative estimates of the assemblies at some places were in the hundreds of thousands. Thus the demonstration at Kersall Moor was reported to have been made up of not less than three hundred thousand; at West Riding of two hundred thousand; at Glasgow of one hundred and thirty thousand, and at Newcastle-on-Tyne of one hundred thousand persons. The meetings were addressed by members of the Convention, including O'Connor, Bronterre, Harney, Frost, and other Chartist celebrities. In several instances the demonstrations were held in defiance of the authorities, who not only refused the requests of the arrangement committees to convene the meetings, but caused proclamations to be posted warning the people against attending illegal gatherings. Everything went off peaceably, although the speakers were by no means timid in the expression of their sentiments. At the West Riding demonstration, O'Connor declared that if the "tyrants" attempted to put down the meeting by force, the people should repel attack by attack. Bronterre did not mince words at any of the meetings, always impressing the people with the necessity of being prepared to do something *effective* for universal suffrage. He upbraided the people for supporting " the whole tribe of landholders, fundholders, and two millions of menials and kept mistresses, together with one hundred thousand prostitutes in London alone ". The speeches by the other agitators were in similar vein.

The Convention reassembled at Birmingham on the 1st of July and immediately took up the question of adjourning to London, as the Birmingham authorities were evidently determined to interfere with its business, having sworn in three hundred special constables that very day. Another reason for the removal was the alleged precarious condition of the Bank of England, which made it strategically advisable for the Convention to be in close touch with the situation in order to avail itself of the embarrassment on the part of the government. On the next day, after a long discussion, it was agreed that the sessions be removed to London on the 10th of that month.

The reports of the delegates on the results of the *simultaneous* meetings showed that, notwithstanding the popular enthusiasm for the Charter, the " ulterior measures " were not approved *en bloc* by the people. The " sacred month " proposition met with decided opposition in all parts of the country. There seemed to be diversity of opinion on this question even among the leaders. In spite of that, however, unanimous resolutions were adopted approving exclusive dealing with Chartists, a run on the banks, absolute abstinence from excisable drinks, and, in view of the expected division on the National Petition which was to take place in Parliament on the 12th of July, it was decided that the members of the Convention meet on the 13th, " for the purpose of appointing a day when the sacred month shall commence, if the Charter has not previously become the law of the land ".

CHAPTER XI

THE WRESTLING FORCES

> Though tyrants and minions reject our prayer,
> And sneer at the evils we patiently bear,
> And laugh us to scorn when we humbly ask,—
> How soon they may have another task!
> At last a smothered fire forth may break,
> And a nation in knowledge of freedom awake.
> —*Alfred Owen Fennell.*

THE simultaneous meetings and the subsequent adoption by the Convention of the " ulterior measures " were followed by a new series of events, in which both the Chartists and the government displayed a mood to fight to the bitter end, and which culminated in temporary victory for the latter.

The first serious encounter between the people and the authorities took place on the 4th of July, 1839, at Birmingham. Since the days of the agitation for the Reform Bill, the people had been accustomed to assemble in vast multitudes in the Bull Ring, where they not only aired their grievances but also listened to the reading of newspapers and discussed political events. The simultaneous meetings struck terror to the hearts of the middle class, and the mayor undertook to restrain the masses from holding public meetings in the city, and particularly in the popular Ring. The resentment of the workingmen against this infringement upon their rights was on a par with their hostility towards the newly-introduced metropolitan police. Nevertheless, no open conflict occurred until the mayor attempted to enforce his proclamation. On the evening stated, a squad of the metropolitan police, headed by the mayor and a magistrate and supported by several detachments of dragoons, invaded the Ring where an assembly of workingmen listened to the reading of a newspaper, and, without any provocation on the part of the people, commenced an indiscriminate attack.   In the confusion, men, women, and children were thrown down and trampled upon, the police belaboring them right and left.   One man had his teeth knocked out, and several were carried away with broken heads and arms and other severe injuries.   After the first moments of panic, the people rallied their strength and compelled the police to flee.   But the latter soon returned, reinforced, and renewed the attack.   The mayor then read the Riot Act, ordered the dragoons to disperse the crowds, and placed military guards at all the avenues leading to the Bull Ring in order to prevent any new gathering there. The fight lasted from nine to half-past ten in the evening. About midnight the dispersed crowds gathered again, singing the Chartist anthem, " Fall, Tyrants, Fall," and amidst deafening cheers proceeded for Holloway Head, in the outskirts of the city, where they swore vengeance against the assailants.   They then marched to St. Thomas's Church, where they tore down about seventy feet of railing and turned it into weapons.   A rush to the scene of the conflict, which might have proven fatal to many, was averted by two popular members of the Convention, Dr. Taylor and McDouall, who induced the incensed people to throw down their improvised arms.

A spirit of terror and vengeance pervaded the city, the fury of the people clashing with the severity of the authorities.   About six o'clock the following morning, Dr. Taylor, together with ten other Chartists, was committed to Warwick jail.   It goes without saying that the " People's Parliament " deemed it its duty to express indignation over the conduct of the authorities, and the following resolutions were adopted and ordered to be placarded on the walls of the city: [1]

1. That this Convention is of opinion that a wanton, flagrant, and unjust outrage has been made upon the people of Birmingham, by a blood-thirsty and unconstitutional force from London, acting under the authority of men, who, when out of office, sanctioned and took part in the meetings of the people; and now, when they share in the public plunder, seek to keep the people in social and political degradation.

2. That the people of Birmingham are the best judges of their own right to meet in the Bull Ring or elsewhere; have their own feelings to consult respecting outrage given, and are the best judges of their own power and resources to obtain justice.

3. That the summary and despotic arrest of Dr. Taylor, our respected colleague, affords another convincing proof of all absence of justice in England, and clearly shows that there is no security for lives, liberty, or property, till the people have some control over the laws they are called upon to obey.

No sooner had the resolutions been posted about the town than the printer was arrested. He was, however, liberated immediately after naming John Collins, a Birmingham local preacher and a member of the Convention, as the person who had ordered the printing. Lovett, who, as secretary, had signed the resolutions, and Collins were speedily arrested and brought up for examination. Both refused to incriminate any other person and were committed for trial at the next assizes. Pending the production of unusually high bail of £1000 each, they were kept for nine days in the county jail of Warwick, the magistrates rais-

---

[1] See *The Trial of William Lovett for a Seditious Libel*, London, 2d edition. *Cf.* also Hansard, *op. cit.*, vol. xlix, 1839, pp. 109-10, and pp. 375-6.

ing every possible objection to the bail offered, and were subjected to the discipline and indignities of convicted felons.[1]

The ire of the masses was intensified by the proclamation of martial law and the conduct of the police, who paraded the streets and dealt brutally with every person that aroused their suspicion. Far from intimidating the workingmen, the wholesale arrests provoked utmost defiance. Instigated by advocates of physical force,[2] large crowds met daily at Holloway Head and other places, serious collisions with the police and military forces resulting. The desultory fights continued for a whole week, and culminated in the second Bull Ring riot on the 15th of July. A number of houses belonging to men who had made themselves obnoxious to the masses were set afire. In their fury, the people entered shops, carried the goods to the Bull Ring, and committed them to the devouring flames. The police and the military were utterly helpless. But not for a minute did the rioters forget the real object of their revolt.

Amid all these desperate proceedings,—Gammage testifies,—the people exhibited a disinterestedness worthy of all imitation. Not even the most costly goods for a moment tempted their cupidity. They even trod under foot the splendid silver plate of Mr. Horton, proving that, however great their provocation, plunder was not their object. They were at war with the ruling classes, but they scorned to avail themselves of the common privileges of warriors. That they had become desperate was not their fault; their vices belonged to their

[1] Referring to these indignities, Lord Brougham stated and reiterated in the House of Lords that the facts were verified "by a most respectable individual, whose cross-examination he would trust as much as that of any man not connected with the legal profession." See Hansard, *op. cit.*, vol. xlix, pp. 438-9 and 984-5.

[2] Holyoake writes that he saw Harney "daily in the riot-week standing at the door openly." See Holyoake, *op. cit.*, vol. i, p. 85.

oppressors, their virtues were their own. Meetings continued to be held, to which the people flocked in crowds. The process of trade was stopped, and a large number of gentry fled the town; even the valiant mayor was terrified into flight.[1]

The conduct of the metropolitan police and the consequent riots in Birmingham were the objects of parliamentary enquiries in both Houses,[2] in which the government was severely criticized. The physical-force agitators also did their best to kindle the passions of the people. Public meetings were held in a large number of cities, and hundreds of resolutions were adopted and printed in the Chartist papers, charging the authorities with high treason to the Constitution. The Northampton resolution threatened the Whig government that it would " be held responsible for the consequences, even if the suffering people . . . should leave at midnight their miserable homes in a blaze, and the destructive element communicating with everything around, reduce to one common ruin and desolation the mansions of the rich and the hovels of the poor." [3]

In the meantime, amidst these disquieting circumstances, the Parliamentary battle for the National Petition was lost by Attwood and his supporters.[4] On the 12th of July, Attwood brought forward his motion that the House resolve itself into a committee for considering the prayer of the National Petition which he had presented on the 14th of June. The anticipation of pungent discussion attracted large crowds. According to Disraeli, " the Tories, supposing Chartism would be only a squabble between the Whigs and Radicals, were all away, while the ministerial benches

---

[1] Gammage, op. cit., p. 135.

[2] See Hansard, op. cit., vol. xlix, pp. 109-111, 410-411 and 441-442.

[3] Gammage, op. cit., p. 138.

[4] See Hansard, op. cit., vol. xlix, pp. 220-256.

were crowded—all the ministers, all the Whigs, and all the Radicals " in their seats.[1]

True to himself, Attwood expounded the Petition from the point of view not only of the working class, but also of the merchants, manufacturers, tradesmen and farmers. He based his appeal on ancient practice of common justice and humanity, as well as actual grounds of utility. Alluding to the petitioners as the elite of the working class, he cautioned the House, however, not to treat the prayer as representing the sentiments merely of that class, for he was certain that the feelings of nine out of every ten persons of the middle class were in full accord with the objects of the Petition. There was, no doubt, " some property " left in England, but, generally speaking, the merchant and the manufacturer, being on the brink of bankruptcy, were not less discontented than the laborers. The people were desirous of a change, and nothing would satisfy them but some large and generous measure. This measure was proposed in the People's Charter. He had always deprecated violence, but he considered it his duty to tell the House that " if the hands of the people were not to be set free from their trammels, if they were not to have the benefit of earning their bread by the sweat of their brow, and hundreds of thousands were compelled to beg for labor and then to be denied bread,—it was his rooted conviction that the people of England would not submit to it and that there was no army in the world capable of putting them down."

The philanthropic but characterless speech of Attwood made the reply of his principal opponent, Lord Russell, appear far more convincing. As the Lord viewed the matter, the whole movement had been promoted by persons who had been going through the country and, in the most revo-

[1] See *Lord Beaconsfield's Correspondence with his Sister*, 1832-1852, edited by Ralph Disraeli, 2d edition, 1886, p. 132.

lutionary language, " not exceeded in violence and atrocity
in the worst times of the French Revolution," exhorted
the people to subvert the laws by force of arms. Having
scored on this point of fact which no one could deny, but
offering no explanation for the generous welcome which the
people had accorded those agitators, he proceeded to de-
molish the fundamental principle of the Charter. He
scorned the idea that universal suffrage or any legal provision relating to representation would establish general
welfare " in a country depending very much upon commerce and manufactures " and prevent that state of low
wages and consequent distress which occur in every community of that kind. Even the United States, where the
people enjoyed universal suffrage, had not been altogether
free from alternate fluctuations from prosperity to distress,
notwithstanding the immense tracts of wild fertile land in
which the population that could not subsist in towns might
easily find refuge and a mode of living. He denied that
the Petition which had only about one million two hundred
thousand signatures was a *national* petition and that it represented the sentiments and opinions of a majority of the
people. On the contrary, the great majority of the nation,
including the working class, would be alarmed at the prospect of having the principles of the Charter enacted into
law. He further referred to the increase of small deposits
in savings' banks as proving the absolute want of truth in
the statement of the Petition that the home of the artificer was desolate and the manufactory deserted. He
did not deny that there were many industrious and sober
workingmen whose means were exceedingly scanty and
whose situation could not be looked upon without com-
miseration. But he was utterly relentless in showing up
the " complete delusion " of those who believed that the
adoption of universal suffrage would place the laborers in

a state of prosperity. Referring to Attwood's pet theory
that the alteration in the standard of value and an increase
in the quantity of paper money would assure general prosperity, the speaker did not fail to point out, not without
ill-concealed sarcasm, that the Chartist leaders and members
of the General Convention had denounced the influence of
paper money as one of the most abominable weapons in the
hands of their oppressors. He stated and reiterated his
opinion that the Petition contained the exhortations chiefly
of " very designing and insidious persons, wishing not the
prosperity of the people," but seeking to arouse discord and
confusion, " to produce a degree of misery, the consequence
of which would be to create a great alarm that would be
fatal, not only to the constitution as it now exists, not only
to those rights which are now said to be monopolized by a
particular class, but fatal to any established government."

Disraeli put it remarkably well when in the course of his
retort to Russell he remarked that " the noble Lord had
answered the speech of the honorable member for Birmingham, but he had not answered the Chartists." It was his
opinion that Attwood had made a very dexterous speech " in
favor of the middle classes," but that actual facts led to a
very different conclusion. He found among the Chartists
the greatest hostility to the middle classes. Stanch Tory
that he was, he discovered that the people " complained only
of the government by the middle classes. They made no
attack on the aristocracy — none on the Corn Laws — but
upon the newly-enfranchised constituency, not on the old—
upon that peculiar constituency which was the basis of the
noble Lord's government." Not committing himself on the
real issues of the Charter, he called to account the Minister
of the Crown for his nonchalant attitude towards the " remarkable social movement " and for despising the one million two hundred and eighty thousand fellow-subjects who

had signed the Petition because of their discontent with the existing conditions. He saw " social insurrection " at the very threshold, and, much as he disapproved of the Charter, he sympathized with the Chartists, who formed a great body of his countrymen and who labored under great grievances.[1]

The debate, in which several other members participated, concluded with the division of forty-eight votes in favor as over against two hundred and thirty-seven in opposition to Attwood's motion.

This division greatly disheartened the Chartist leaders. The Convention, which had reconvened in London on the 10th of July, fully realized how serious a blow the cause had received, as well as its own impotence which resulted from the arrest and resignation of many of its members. On the day after the defeat of Attwood's motion, being of the opinion that it was utterly useless to expect anything from the House by way of petitioning, and that the people would not get liberty until they *took* it, the question of a general strike, or a *sacred month*, was again brought up for consideration. After lengthy discussions, a resolution was finally passed on the 16th that it was the opinion of the Convention " that the people should work no longer after the 12th of August next, unless the power of voting for members of parliament, to protect their labor, is guaranteed to them." This resolution was, however, subsequently rescinded on the motion of Bronterre, who stated that strict enquiries of the leaders in various districts had convinced him that the people were not prepared to carry out a general strike. Letters to the same effect were also read from Frost and other leaders. The painful consciousness of lack

---

[1] Disraeli himself called this " a capital speech " and seemed to have taken pride in the fact that the Whig government did not like it. See the same letter quoted above.

of authority on the part of the Convention was revealed in the following resolution which was introduced by Bronterre and carried by a vote of twelve against six, the remaining seven members present refusing to commit themselves: [1]

That while the Convention continues to be unanimously of opinion that nothing short of a general strike, or suspension of labor throughout the country, will ever suffice to re-establish the rights and liberties of the industrious classes, we nevertheless cannot take upon ourselves the responsibility of dictating the time or circumstances of such strike, believing that we are incompetent to do so for the following reasons:

1st: Because our numbers have been greatly reduced by the desertion, absence, and arbitrary arrests of a large portion of our members.

2nd: Because great diversity of opinion prevails amongst the remaining members, as to the practicability of a general strike, in the present state of trade in the manufacturing districts.

3rd: Because a similar diversity of opinion seems to prevail out of doors, amongst our constituents and the working classes generally.

4th: Because, under these circumstances, it is more than doubtful whether an order from the Convention for a general holiday would not be a failure.

5th: Because, while we firmly believe that an universal strike would prove the salvation of the country, we are at the same time equally convinced that a partial strike would only entail the bitterest privations and sufferings on all parties who take part in it, and, in the present exasperated state of public feeling, not improbably lead to confusion and anarchy.

6th: Because, although it is the duty of the Convention to participate in all the people's dangers, it is no part of our duty to create danger unnecessarily, either for ourselves or others.

[1] Gammage, *op. cit.*, p. 146.

To create it for ourselves would be folly—to create it for others would be a crime.

7th: Because we believe that the people themselves are the only fit judges of their right and readiness to strike work, as also of their own resources and capabilities of meeting the emergencies which such an event would entail. Under these circumstances, we decide that a committee of three be appointed to reconsider the vote of the 16th instant, and to substitute for it an address, which shall leave to the people themselves to decide whether they will or will not commence the sacred month on the 12th of August, at the same time explaining the reasons for adopting such a course, and pledging the Convention to co-operate with the people in whatever measures they may deem necessary to their safety and emancipation.

The committee provided for in the resolution was extended to five members, and included Bronterre and O'Connor. The evidence collected with reference to the expediency of a general strike convinced them that such a step would be fatal to the movement, and they unanimously recommended the abandonment of the project of a sacred month. On the 6th of August a resolution to the same effect, moved by Bronterre and seconded by O'Connor, was accordingly passed by the General Council of the Convention, recommending at the same time the cessation of work *for two or three days* " in order to devote the whole of that time to solemn processions and solemn meetings." The resolution embodied a strong appeal to all the trades to coöperate as united bodies in making a grand national moral demonstration on the 12th of August, as otherwise " it will be impossible to save the country from a revolution of blood, which after enormous sacrifices of life and property will terminate in the utter subjection of the working people to the monied murderers of society."

The lack of organization and centralized leadership was

keenly felt at this critical period, and the "national holiday" turned out a complete fiasco, causing some disturbances in several towns, but generally unobserved throughout
the country.   Its original self-confidence and aggressiveness
having disappeared, the Convention could hardly expect to
have its mandates respected by the Chartists at large.   The
"People's Parliament" thus lost its *raison d'être*.   Bronterre's motion on the 6th of September for the dissolution of
the body, however, met stringent opposition, and the members being equally divided—eleven against eleven—it was
carried only by the deciding vote of the chairman.   The
division was by no means on party lines, some of the extreme revolutionists voting with the most devoted followers
of Lovett.

The dissolution of the Convention came at a time when
the government policy of persecution and terror had assumed unparalleled proportions.   Hundreds of Chartists
had been arrested and tried for sedition, and no relaxation
was in view.   Severe sentences were imposed on national
and local leaders, in accordance with the theory of the
Attorney-General that there was danger in allowing those
men of talent to be at large.   The government first showed
its mettle on the 5th and 6th of August, at the trial of
Lovett and Collins for seditious libel.   The attack on the
Bull Ring assembly had been made, as Lovett said in his
defence, "the subject of reprehension and censure from
one extremity of the kingdom to another."   The public enquiry of the Town Council of Birmingham showed that the
universal condemnation was well founded.   In its resolution the Council used practically the same terms for which
Lovett and Collins were tried.   The enquiry "proved that
a brutal and bloody attack had been made upon the people
of Birmingham, and that it was their opinion that if the
police had not attacked the people, no disorder would have

occurred, and they considered the riot was incited by the London police." [1]

Notwithstanding these facts, the Government did its utmost to convict Lovett and his colleague, ostensibly for the resolutions on the Bull-Ring outrage but in reality for the rôle which these victims had played in the General Convention. The prosecutor dwelt at length on the document which Lovett had signed by order of the Convention "with all the form and solemnity of a proclamation by Her Majesty Queen Victoria," and said bluntly that " the Attorney-General would have neglected his duty if he had not selected for prosecution Mr. Lovett, who was a man of very considerable powers. He was a man who, if he willed to do ill, had the capacity to do it." [2]   The men selected to serve on the jury were decidedly hostile to the defendants, two of them having previously avowed their conviction that " all Chartists ought to be hanged." The objection of Lovett to those men was of no avail. Collins was defended by Sergeant Goulburn, a prominent Tory, who saw in his task, as he expressed it, " a glorious opportunity of having a slap at the Whigs." Lovett conducted his own defence, disregarding the adage quoted to him by his friends that " he who defends himself has a fool for his client." He delivered a masterly address to the jury in a manner which strongly contrasted with the political speech of the professional advocate Goulburn. Surveying the history and the causes that had led to the Chartist movement, he asserted in a dignified and convincing way the constitutional right of public meetings, of free discussion, and of public petitioning. The Chartist movement, as all other movements in favor of the oppressed, necessarily occasioned great un-

[1] Lovett, op. cit., p. 220.

[2] The Trial of William Lovett for a Seditious Libel, 2d edition, London, pp. 5 and 19.

easiness among those who would be deprived of unjust power and corrupt privilege. Far greater culpability was on the side of those who instigated the Bull Ring disorder than on the part of the people who merely repulsed the flagrant and unconstitutional attack. The resolutions which he had signed were perfectly justified by the circumstances. He refuted the charge of criminal intention on his part, and quoted many authorities, political and legal, to substantiate his arguments as to the lack of guilt from a technical, as well as from a moral, point of view. In its comments on the trial, the *Morning Chronicle* of August 8, 1839, said:

The speeches of Mr. Sergeant Goulburn, in defence of John Collins, and William Lovett in his own defence, present an edifying contrast of tone and temper—of taste and judgment. The learned sergeant's argument, had he made it out, could have little profited his client, or served the ends of justice. Had that of Mr. Lovett been better supported by facts, it must have secured his acquittal. The one is a misplaced ebullition of party virulence; the other a temperate and talented pleading, which elicited strong commendation from the counsel for the prosecution. And yet the one of these men, independently of his professional standing, was long deemed one of the principal supporters of his party in the House of Commons, while *the other has not even a voice in the election of a representative to sit in that House.* Is it strange that Mr. Lovett should be a discontented man? We condemn the language for which he has been convicted; we should also condemn him were he satisfied to belong to what Mr. Hume emphatically calls the "slave class." *His defence at least demonstrates his qualification for the franchise.*

Lovett's appeal for a favorable verdict was an impassioned plea for the rights of man. But it fell on deaf ears. It took the jury but two or three minutes of deliberation to return a verdict of "guilty," and the defendants were each

sentenced to twelve months' imprisonment. This singular
victory of the government prosecutor was followed by a
number of others. The prediction of the terrorists came
true, and the authorities looked " upon all parties in the
Chartist ranks alike." Adherents of either wing were
seized and punished severely for most trivial offences.
Even Stephens, who at his trial, on the 15th of August, repudiated all radicalism, was sentenced to imprisonment for
a period of eighteen months. Four Chartists were sentenced to death for participation in the Bull Ring outbreak,
and it was only after strong representations to the government that their punishment was commuted to transportation for life. Within a very short period there was hardly
a leader who was not committed to jail or not bound to
appear for trial.

The breaking-up of the Convention did not in the least
affect the mood of the ardent supporters of the Charter.
Public meetings and open demonstrations gave place to
more dangerous vehicles of agitation within narrow circles
of revengeful conspirators. The ill-feeling of the workingmen grew ever more ominous because of the inexorable
rigor and discipline to which the Chartist prisoners were
subjected. Lovett and Collins, the least offensive of the
agitators, soon found out that it was impossible for them
to preserve their health on the kind of food allowed to them
and begged, but in vain, to be permitted to purchase a little
tea, sugar and butter, and occasionally a small quantity of
meat. The magistrates also refused to allow them, without
specific authority from the Secretary of State, the use of
writing materials and books. Petitions and memorials in
their favor were presented by the Working Men's Association, the people of Birmingham, Francis Place, and members of Parliament. But, as Lovett states, whenever the
magistrates were applied to for any little mitigation of their

severities, "they invariably contended that they had no power without the sanction of the Secretary of State; and when he was memorialized, he referred us to the visiting magistrates." [1]   Other Chartists, without the powerful influence exerted on behalf of Lovett and his colleague, were entirely at the mercy of the wrathful prison authorities, and some of the victims subsequently died in jail from diseases contracted there.

The policy of retaliation pursued by the government towards the Chartist prisoners caused particular resentment in the case of Henry Vincent, the idol of the Welsh miners, who was tried on the 2d of August, and sentenced to imprisonment in Monmouth county jail for a period of twelve months.   The open hostility of the jury, one of whom had been heard to declare that *he would give nine-pence to buy a halter for hanging the defendant without judge or jury*, and the severe punishment, caused much acrimony against the authorities.   The treatment of the prisoner like a common felon still more irritated his admirers.   Frost himself, on the 28th of September, wrote to a former colleague, a magistrate of the county, exhorting him to obtain a mitigation of Vincent's treatment.   All remonstrances and protests, however, were of no avail.   It was then that the Welsh Chartists conceived the idea of releasing Vincent by force and began to perfect plans which culminated in the Newport Riot of November 4, 1839, when thousands of men " rushed like a torrent from the hills," armed with the gun, the pike, and the bludgeon, " to lay in ruins the commercial emporium of their county."

[1] Lovett, *op. cit.*, pp. 229-231.

CHAPTER XII

THE NEWPORT RIOT

THE stories of the events leading to the Welsh rising are utterly conflicting. The biographer of John Frost denies the existence of any previous plan of organization:

Those who have said that Mr. Frost was long engaged in organizing the people for the Newport outbreak, must hereafter hold their peace, or be content to have attached to them the imputation of uttering against a man who has it not in power to defend himself, an injurious allegation, which there exists no evidence to establish . . . The gathering on the eve of the riots *had no direct object laid down*, and that, until a very few hours previous to their meeting, the assembly was not even agreed upon.[1]

Lovett, on the other hand, gives what seems to be a more authentic account, obtained " from a person who took an active part in matters pertaining to it." It appears that, having failed in his endeavors on behalf of Vincent, Frost came to London and confided to two or three members of the Convention his great difficulty in restraining the Welsh Chartists from attempting to release the prisoner by force. One of the conferees then gave assurance that if the Welsh effected a rising in favor of Vincent, the people of Yorkshire and Lancashire would join in a rising for the Charter. The parties decided not to take any steps before consulting the local leaders in their respective districts. Shortly afterwards a meeting was held at Heckmondwick which was

[1] *The Life of John Frost, Esq.*, London, 1840, p. 7.

attended by about forty delegates, including three members of the Convention, and which expressed a determination to aid the intended rising in Wales by a simultaneous outbreak in the North. O'Connor was requested by a special Yorkshire delegate to lead them, and was apparently misunderstood by the latter, who reported the leader's readiness to head the rising. Finding that the people were in earnest, he immediately sent one representative to Yorkshire and Lancashire and another to Wales to caution the leaders against the rising. When found by O'Connor's envoy, Frost informed him that the message came too late, that the people were resolved on releasing Vincent from prison, and that he might as well blow his own brains out as try to oppose them or shrink back. He urged him to go back to the North and inform the leaders of the Welsh preparations. The riot, however, was precipitated before any outside aid could be rendered.[1]

The activities of Frost before the outbreak in no way tended to allay the spirit of strife. His last public letter, dated at Newport, October 22, 1839, and addressed to the farmers and tradesmen of Monmouthshire, assumes particular significance in the light of the subsequent tragic insurrection. Assuring his " fellow-countrymen " that, unless the Charter be speedily enacted, " there will be no security for person or property," the author seeks to impress the people with the realization of the cause of such unsafety:

In all countries, where great discontent has existed, there

---

[1] *Cf.* Lovett, *op. cit.*, pp. 239-241. In his enmity towards O'Connor, Lovett never fails to impeach the conduct and motives of the latter. In this case, he insinuates that O'Connor misleadingly induced " the poor fellow," the Yorkshire delegate, to believe that he would head the insurrection, as well as that he " set about to render the outbreak ineffectual."

always must have been a cause, and that cause always was the oppression and cruelty of men in authority. What is it which has rendered the laboring classes of this country so discontented? What has produced that deep and powerful feeling which a spark would now ignite from one end of the country to the other? A deep sense of wrong—a thorough conviction of the injustice with which they are treated. Their labor is taken from them by the means of the law; it is given to a set of idle and dissolute men and women; those who produce not, are clothed in purple and fine linen, and fare sumptuously every day, while the laborer is fed with the crumbs which fall from the table of the rich. The working-men have petitioned for justice; their petitions were treated with contempt, and their leaders imprisoned and treated with greater severity than felons; they ask for a reduction of taxation, and the answer is, a rural police.

The proceedings of the last Quarter Sessions, are well worthy your serious attention. One oppressive act follows the other. Sometime ago we had a Poor-law Amendment Act, by which the management of your own money was completely taken out of your own hands, and placed in the hands of the landlords. Here's a pretty law, by which poverty is made a crime and punished by confinement, by a separation of man and wife, and parent and child. To support this oppressive law we are now to have a rural police!—armed men all over the country—to suppress discontent by force, and the murmurings of poverty by the bludgeon! And this, too, in England —in the land formerly of freedom—in the land in which, at one time, the constable's staff, and the sheriff's wand, were quite sufficient to preserve peace. . . .

Suppose the farmers and tradesmen were to ask themselves how is this likely to end? It must produce one of two states of things. Every year will add to the oppression and poverty of the people. Tyranny has no cessation; every desperate act must be supported by one more violent, the preservation of the tyrants renders this necessary. We are fast approaching the state of France, previously to the first revolution. We have spies watching all public proceedings; every word will very soon be weighed in the balance of the despot, and construed at the will of those in authority. This will produce a sullen discontent which will be evinced in a way to render property and life insecure. This will be a pretty state of society when every farmer will come to market with a brace of pistols in his pocket—when every man in authority will be looking for an enemy in every one he meets. This is no imaginary picture, it will be a state of society, the natural effects of taxation, of poverty, of misery, and of crime.

Look at the other side of the picture; suppose that the working-men, driven to despair, should follow the example of our own, and of other, countries. Here would be a state of suffering! All the angry passions in full scope—resentment for past injuries, hatred public and private. Where, in such a case, would be the voice that, under those circumstances, would be listened to? The French people, previously to the revolution, were led by some of the most benevolent men in the world; they sought for a change in the most oppressive laws that ever existed. The government fancied that if it could destroy the leaders, that all would be well. In many instances it succeeded; and what was the consequence? Leaders ten times more violent. It appears to be the opinion of the authorities in this country, that if they could imprison or destroy the leaders of the movement, that all would be well. Never was there a greater mistake. Could they succeed, they would exchange benevolent men for cruel ones. Stopping the movement is out of the question, unless by altering a system which is the cause of all the evils of which the people complain.[1]

The plan of the Welsh Chartists, as brought out at the subsequent trials, was to have the members of the various lodges throughout the district assemble, fully armed, and then march towards Newport in three divisions. A copy of

---

[1] *The English Chartist Circular*, no. 27.

the directions produced at the magistrates' examinations gave the details of the scheme: [1]

Let us form into sections, by choosing a good staunch independent brother at the head of each section; that is to say, each section to be composed of ten men, who are known to him to be sincere, so that the head of each section may know his men. Thus five sections will comprise 55 men and officers. Then these five officers—such as corporals—will choose a head officer, so that he may give his five officers notice; so these 50 men are to be called a bye-name; then three fifties will compose a company, and the three officers will choose a proper person to command the 165 in company, officers and all, such as a captain. Then three companies will compose 495 men and officers, which officer will be such as a brigade-general. So three brigades will choose a chief, which will be 1485 men and officers, which chief officer is to be in the style of a conventional-general. So that by these means the signal "W. R." can be given in two hours' notice, within seven miles, by the head officer noticing every officer under him, until it comes to the deacons or corporals to notice their ten men; the officers to have bye-names—not military names.

It was decided that the first division, starting from Blackwood, should be headed by Frost; the second, composed of men from Brynmawr and Ebbw Vale, should leave the latter place under the command of Zephaniah Williams; while the third division, consisting of the Chartists from Blaenavon, Abersychan, and neighboring places, should leave Pontypool under the leadership of William Jones. [2]

[1] *The Chartist Riots at Newport, November, 1839*, 2d edition, 1889, pp. 19-20.

[2] Zephaniah Williams, a keeper of a beerhouse in a little town near Newport, was one of the most enthusiastic followers of Vincent and Frost, and during the Chartist agitation exercised great influence among the workingmen of his district.

William Jones, or William Lloyd Jones, as he designated himself in later years, was the illegitimate son of a tradesman at Bristol. In his

The three divisions were directed to meet on Sunday, November the third, at midnight, at a place several miles from Newport.   Thence they would march into the town, which would be reached about two o'clock in the morning, attack the troops who were expected to be caught unprepared in the absence of any suspicion of danger, break down the bridge across the Usk, stop the mail-coaches and the traffic, and take possession of the town.   The delay of the mail was to be a signal to Birmingham, and then to the whole North, to rise in arms.

The plan was carried out only in part.   On the Sunday preceding the attack, all villages in the district were in a state of mobilization, and, in spite of the heavy rain, men of all ages, fathers and sons, gathered at the appointed places, armed with weapons of every description.   Those who had known nothing of the plot were struck with terror and hid themselves in the recesses of their dwellings or in the neighboring woods.   Many houses are reported to have been searched, and men dragged from bed and forced to join the march.   The center of all action was in Blackwood, where the commander-in-chief, John Frost, issued orders and received reports from his subordinates. About seven o'clock a messenger presented himself to Frost, saying that he had come from Newport; that " the soldiers there were in the barracks; that they were all Chartists; that their arms and ammunition were all packed, and that they were all ready to come up on the Hills, only they were waiting for the Chartists to go down to fetch them." [1]

youth he gave up his trade of watchmaker and became a strolling actor. In 1833 he was made the manager of a watchmaking business in Pontypool, and then, after his marriage, started the same business on his own account. His attractive personality and histrionic talents rendered him a commanding figure among the Pontypool Chartists.   In the movement he distinguished himself as one of the most zealous advocates of physical force.

[1] *The Chartist Riots at Newport*, p. 21.

This was evidently a spurious report. As a matter of fact, the news had by that time reached Newport that the Chartists were scouring the Hills in all directions and gathering great forces. The mayor, Thomas Phillips, immediately summoned five hundred special constables and stationed them in various places. Messengers and scouts were sent out in all directions to watch and report the progress of the Chartist movements. In his intense alarm at the news imparted to him by the spies, the mayor also despatched a request to Bristol that a reinforcement of troops be sent at once to Newport. In the course of the evening special constables paraded the streets and arrested all suspicious persons.

The severity of the weather and the incessant torrents of rain during the whole night greatly impeded the progress of the several divisions, which more than once had to seek shelter. Thus the original plan of invading Newport at night was completely upset. It was morning when the gathered forces reached the outskirts of the town, and the news of their approach reached the mayor in time for him to station himself with a military detachment and fifty constables in the Westgate Hotel, where a number of prisoners taken during the night were detained. About nine o'clock the head of the Chartist body, under the command of Frost, appeared, cheering and shouting, at the gates of the Westgate Hotel. The men were armed with "guns, pistols, blunderbusses, swords, bayonets, daggers, pikes, bill-hooks, reaping-hooks, hatchets, cleavers, axes, pitch-forks, blades of knives, scythes and saws fixed in staves, pieces of iron two and three yards in length, sharpened at the one end, bludgeons of various length and size, hand and sledge-hammers, mandrils—in fact, every weapon that could be at all made available." [1] The leading ranks made an attempt to enter

---

[1] *The Rise and Fall of Chartism in Monmouthshire*, p. 4.

the stable-yard, but finding the gates strongly barred, they proceeded to the portico of the Hotel. One of the leaders ascended the steps and demanded the surrender of the prisoners, to which a special constable replied, " No, never!" The firing of the first gun, however, dissipated the courage of the constables, who were armed only with staves. Most of them fled, some to the cellars, some to the roof, and others to the yard and other places of security, leaving a few of their wounded comrades to the mercy of the invaders. Within a few moments the house was blockaded by the rebels, who fired frequent shots through the broken windows into the various rooms of the building. It was then that the mayor, slightly wounded, ordered the soldiers to use their guns. The well-aimed volleys soon proved effective. The piercing shrieks of scores of dying and wounded men created a panic which destroyed all discipline in the rear as well as the front ranks. The rebel army, variously estimated between ten and twenty thousand men, recoiled in horror before a mere handful of defenders, scattering their weapons and even their garments as they scampered away in all directions. After ten or fifteen minutes of steady and deadly firing by the soldiers, even the most reckless conspirators fled from the place, which presented a most gruesome sight:

Many who suffered in the fight, crawled away; some exhibiting frightful wounds, and glaring eyes, wildly crying for mercy, and seeking a shelter from the charitable; others, desperately maimed, were carried in the arms of the humane for medical aid; and a few of the miserable objects that were helplessly and mortally wounded, continued for some minutes to writhe in torture, crying for water, and presenting, in their gory agonies, a dismal and impressive example to any of the political seducers, or the seduced, who might have been within view, and a sickening and melancholy spectacle for the eye of humanity.[1]

[1] *The Rise and Fall of Chartism in Monmouthshire*, p. 43.

Inside the Westgate five dead bodies and a number of severely wounded men were found weltering in their blood. One man, who was discovered under the portico of the mayor's house, where he had crept, after receiving a gun-shot wound, expired exclaiming, "The Charter for ever!" Altogether twenty-two bodies were gathered and subsequently interred in St. Woolos churchyard. A characteristic expression of the zealous faith in the cause which impelled the actions of those men even to the extent of martyrdom is found in the letter which one of the victims, a cabinetmaker from Pontypool, a youth barely nineteen years of age, wrote to his parents on the eve of the riot: [1]

Dear Parents:
I hope this will find you well, as I am myself at present. I shall this night be engaged in a struggle for freedom, and should it please God to spare my life, I shall see you soon; but if not, grieve not for me. I shall fall in a noble cause. My tools are at Mr. Cecil's, and likewise my clothes.
Yours truly,
GEORGE SHELL.

In the consternation that followed this attack the authorities did not lose time in taking steps to bring the conspirators to justice. A reward of £100 was offered for the capture of any of the three chief commanders. Frost was taken into custody before the close of the evening. When apprehended, he appeared fatigued and depressed, and surrendered without protest. He handed from his pockets three new pistols, a flask nearly full of powder and about fifty bullets. Jones was arrested about a week after the attack, and Williams eluded capture for ten days. The three leaders and ten other Chartists were committed, and subsequently indicted for high treason, while about thirty

[1] *The Chartist Riots at Newport*, p. 45.

others were held on lesser charges. The attitude of the government left no doubt that the fate of the principal actors was sealed. On the 9th of November, the mayor of Newport received a letter from the Secretary of State for the Home Department, conveying the Queen's approval of his conduct, and this expression of thanks was followed on the 13th with an offer of knighthood for the mayor. The several constables who had been wounded in the affray were rewarded with pensions of £20 per annum each for life. Vincent's paper, *The Western Vindicator*, which had a large circulation among the Welsh workingmen, was seized wherever it could be found, and was suppressed until it disappeared. The Chartists, on the other hand, took up the cause of the prisoners in quite a practical way. A convention represented by many delegates met in London and decided to try all available means to secure a favorable verdict for their comrades, and the appeals for funds by the defense committees throughout the country received generous response.

The Special Commission, which was headed by the Lord Chief Justice Nicholas Tindal, opened its sittings on the 10th of December, 1839, in the Crown Court at Monmouth. The town was in a state of intense excitement. Constabulary and military forces were stationed near and within the court-house, and, in apprehension of all possible contingencies, loop-holes were pierced in the structure in such positions as to enable troops to fire upon any person approaching. The Chief Justice charged the grand jury and defined the law relating to high treason. The next day Frost and twelve of his associates were placed at the bar and informed that a true bill of high treason had been found against them by the grand jury. The indictment comprised four counts, the substance of the charges being that the defendants had broken their faith and true alle-

giance to the Sovereign and levied war against the Queen
within her realm with intent to compel her to change her
measures. The trial commenced on the 31st of December,
when the prisoners pleaded "not guilty," and resolved to
sever in their challenges. The trial of Frost came first.
Both the Attorney-General and the counsel for the defense
contested the case with distinct dexterity and resolve. The
effect of the damaging evidence given by most of the thirty-
seven witnesses could not, however, be destroyed by the
counsel, and on the 8th of January, 1840, after half an
hour's deliberation, the jury brought in a verdict of
"guilty," accompanied by a recommendation of the prisoner "to the merciful consideration of the court." Zephaniah Williams was put on trial on the 9th of January, and
on the 13th the jury returned a verdict of "guilty" with
the same recommendation. The court then proceeded with
the case of William Jones, and an identical verdict was returned on the 15th of the same month. On the following
day the three prisoners were brought in to receive sentence.
Frost appeared calm and resigned; Williams was ghastly
pale and leaned for support against the dock; but Jones
remained firm and dignified to the very last, apparently little
impressed by the solemn import with which the Lord Chief
Justice, holding out no hope of mercy, addressed the convicted Chartists. The latter retained their equanimity even
after the sentence had been pronounced in the following
appalling words:

That you, John Frost, and you, Zephaniah Williams, and
you, William Jones, be taken hence to the place from whence
you came, and be thence drawn on a hurdle to the place of
execution, and that each of you be there hanged by the neck
until you be dead; and that afterwards the head of each of
you shall be severed from his body, and the body of each,
divided into four quarters, shall be disposed of as her Majesty

shall think fit.   And may God almighty have mercy upon your souls.[1]

A similar sentence was subsequently passed upon five other rioters, who had pleaded guilty to the charge of high treason, on the understanding that their lives would be spared. The Chief Justice accordingly intimated to them that, as they had not been the contrivers of the treason, their punishment would be commuted to transportation for life. Of the other prisoners, eighteen were sentenced to various terms of hard labor, while a larger number were either traversed to the assizes or acquitted.

The news of the conviction of the Welsh chieftains was received by the Chartists with an ebullition of wrath. Numerous spontaneous meetings were held throughout the country, protesting against the sentence as a perversion of justice and an act of vengeance, and petitioning both Houses of Parliament to save the lives of the convicts. Memorials praying for mercy were also presented to the Queen. The serious outbreaks in Sheffield, Bradford, and other towns, threatened to spread to the large industrial centers. Rumors of incendiarism began to circulate from town to town. The government, however, seemed not to waver from its determination to carry out the sentence. The possibility of mitigating the penalty caused Sir John Campbell, the Attorney-General, keen mental anguish. He appeared personally to argue against the validity of the objection which had been raised at the trials by the counsel for the defense, and which the Lord Chief Justice had submitted for consideration to the Court of Exchequer, namely, that the lists of witnesses and the jury had not been delivered to the prisoners in pursuance of the Act of Parliament. The case was argued by both sides on the 25th, 27th and 28th of January, and the

---

[1] *The Rise and Fall of Chartism in Monmouthshire*, p. 8a.

Court decided that the objection, although valid, had not been taken at the proper time. The state of mind of Sir Campbell is revealed in the following remarks which he entered in his diary after the conclusion of the trials: [1]

I have passed a very anxious day, as if I myself had been on trial. To my utter astonishment and dismay, Tindal summed up for an acquittal. What he meant, the Lord only knows. No human being doubted the guilt of the accused, and we had proved it by the clearest evidence. Chief Justice Tindal is a very honorable man, and had no assignable reason for deviating from the right course. Yet from the beginning to the end of his charge, he labored for an acquittal.

The execution of the three convicts was fixed for Saturday, February 1, 1840. The executioner, the heads-man, the scaffold, and the implements of death were kept in readiness, when a respite for the prisoners reached Monmouth on the 30th of January. This, however, inspired but little hope, as it was immediately followed by an official announcement of the High Sheriff that the sentence would be carried out on the 6th of February. On January 31st, Sir Frederick Pollock, the chief counsel for Frost, for the sixth time headed a deputation to Lord Melbourne endeavoring to prevail on him to mitigate the severity of the punishment. The Premier remained inflexible, although Sir Pollock had conveyed to him the urgent personal entreaty of Lord Brougham. When informed of the result, the latter persuaded Sir Pollock to try once more. The seventh interview proved successful. Rumors had it that in this decision the government gratified the personal wishes of the Queen. On the 1st of February a respite during Her Majesty's pleasure was read to the prisoners, and secret orders were given to the governor of the jail to be pre-

[1] *The Chartist Riots at Newport*, pp. 66-67.

pared for immediate departure with the convicts. On Sunday night, the 2d of February, Frost, Williams and Jones were removed from Monmouth jail and, under military escort, conveyed to Chepstow and placed on a steamer which was bound for Portsmouth. All efforts to save the victims from banishment proved futile, the Secretary of State holding that he could not, consistently with his public duty, advise the Queen to grant the prayers. On the 24th of the same month the three Welshmen, together with two hundred and ten other prisoners, embarked in a convict vessel at Spithead, destined for Van Diemen's Land. The motion which Representative Leader brought forward on the 10th of March, for an address to the Queen praying for a free pardon, was supported only by seven members.[1]

While the doom of the banished leaders continued to agitate the minds of the Chartists, sincere sympathy was everywhere expressed to the relatives of the men slain at the Westgate. On Sunday, April 12, 1840, the graves of the victims were decorated with flowers and laurels, surmounted with the following lines:

> May the rose of England never blow,
> The Clyde of Scotland cease to flow,
> The harp of Ireland never play,
> Until the Chartists gain the day.

[1] The repeated agitation on behalf of the three martyrs finally led the government, in 1854, to grant them conditional pardons, forbidding return to the United Kingdom. Frost went to the United States, where he resided for two years. The numerous memorials from Newport, Sheffield, and other towns, finally won him unconditional pardon. In August, 1856, he returned to Newport, and was received with great enthusiasm. The Town Council, however, refused to comply with his demand to have his name restituted in the list of freemen of the borough. He then took up his residence at Stapleton. After years of seclusion, he died on the 28th of July, 1877.

Williams, who had become a wealthy coal owner, died on the 8th of May, 1874, in Tasmania.

Jones pursued his occupation of watchmaker at Launceston, Australia, having no desire to go elsewhere. He died there in December, 1873.

The onslaught of the government was not confined to Wales alone. The prosecutions of the Chartists filled the chronicles of well-nigh every town in the United Kingdom. The outrages of the police and the spies became a public nuisance. One after another the active men in the movement were apprehended and convicted. Most of the leaders conducted their own defense, and their addresses to the jury, some of them lasting five, six and even ten hours, became a singular feature at these trials. Severe penalties were imposed on Bronterre, O'Connor, the veteran radical William Benbow, and other leaders, and all were subjected to the most humiliating treatment by the prison authorities.

The following table shows the distribution of the Chartist prisoners confined for various terms for seditious libel, for riot, for attending illegal meetings, for possession of arms, and other political offences, from January 1, 1839, to June 1, 1840 :[1]

CHARTIST CONVICTS IN ENGLAND

County.	Where Confined.	Number of Convicts.
Chester	County Gaol	29
Durham	County Gaol	3
Kent	House of Correction, Canterbury	1
Lancaster	Lancaster Castle	5
	County Gaol and House of Correction, Kirkdale	135
	House of Correction, Preston	3
Lincoln	Lincoln Castle	1
Middlesex	House of Correction	14
	Gaol of Newgate	8
	Westminster Bridewell	13
Monmouth	County Gaol	63
	House of Correction, Usk	4
Northumberland	House of Correction, Newcastle	19

[1] Based on returns to an order of the House of Commons. *Cf. The English Chartist Circular*, no. 1.

Nottingham	County Gaol	23
	House of Correction, Southwell	12
Somerset	County Gaol, Ilchester	3
Surrey	Queen's Bench Prison	2
Warwick	County Gaol	28
Wilts.............	County Gaol	8
	House of Correction, Devizes	1
Worcester	Gaol and House of Correction	3
York	York Castle	69
	East Riding, House of Correction	2
	North Riding, House of Correction	12
	West Riding, House of Correction	19

Total for England 480

CHARTIST CONVICTS IN WALES

County.	Where Confined.	Number of Convicts.
Brecon	County Gaol and House of Correction	12
Glamorgan	House of Correction, Swansea	1
Montgomery	Gaol and House of Correction	50

Total for Wales 63

Total for England and Wales 543

The wholesale arrests and the ruthless persecution of the Chartists seemed to have crushed the movement. The Whig press had apparent cause to rejoice at the government victory. The excitement caused by the Newport riot and the subsequent trials was gradually waning; public meetings became less frequent and less aggressive, and a large portion of the Chartist press went out of existence. There were all the symptoms of an early death of the monster movement. Yet even then all but those blinded with conceit and self-delusion could see the new weapons that were being forged by the workingmen against their enemies. Carlyle voiced the truth when he said that it was the "chimera of Chartism" and not the reality that was put

down.[1] The causes of discontent remaining unhampered,
the hydra-headed "chimera" could not be crushed. Indeed, the government prosecutor had not completed his task
of heaping vengeance on the organizers of the movement
when a new force of recruits appeared on the battlefield
ready to fight and to win.

But this begins a new chapter in the history of Chartism.

[1] Thomas Carlyle, *Chartism*, London, 1840, p. 2.

APPENDIX A

" To the Honorable the Commons of Great Britain and Ireland. The Petition of the undersigned Members of the Working Men's Association and others sheweth—

" That the only *rational use* of the institutions and laws of
society is justly to protect, encourage, and support all that can
be made to contribute *to the happiness of all the people*.

" That, as the object to be obtained is mutual benefit, so
ought the enactment of laws to be by mutual consent.

" That obedience to laws can only be *justly enforced* on the
certainty that those who are called on to obey them have had,
either personally or by their representatives, a power to enact,
amend, or repeal them.

" That all those who are excluded from this share of political power are not justly included within the operation of the
laws; to them the laws are only despotic enactments, and the
legislative assembly from whom they emanate can only be
considered parties to an unholy compact, devising plans and
schemes for taxing and subjecting the many.

" That the universal political right of every human being is
superior and stands apart from all customs, forms, or ancient
usage; a fundamental right not in the power of man to confer,
or justly to deprive him of.

" That to take away this sacred right from the *person* and
to vest it in *property*, is a wilful perversion of justice and
common sense, as the creation and security of property *are the
consequences of society*—the great object of which is human
happiness.

" That any constitution or code of laws, formed in violation of men's political and social rights, are not rendered sacred by time nor sanctified by custom.

" That the ignorance which originated, or permits their operation, forms no excuse for perpetuating the injustice; nor can aught but force or fraud sustain them, when any considerable number of the people perceive and feel their degradation.

" That the intent and object of your petitioners are to present such facts before your Honorable House as will serve to convince you and the country at large that you do not represent the people of these realms; and to appeal to your sense of right and justice, as well as to every principle of honor, for directly making such legislative enactments as shall cause the mass of the people to be represented; with the view of securing *the greatest amount of happiness to all classes of society.*

" Your petitioners find, by returns ordered by your Honorable House, that the whole people of Great Britain and Ireland are about 24 millions, and that the males above 21 years of age are 6,023,752, who, in the opinion of your petitioners, are justly entitled to the elective right.

" That according to S. Wortley's return (ordered by your Honorable House) the number of registered electors, who have the power to vote for members of Parliament, are only 839,-519, and of this number only 8½ in 12 give their votes.

" That on an analysis of the constituency of the United Kingdom, your petitioners find that 331 members (being a *majority* of your Honorable House) are returned by *one hundred and fifty-one thousand four hundred and ninety-two registered electors!*

" That comparing the whole of the male population above the age of 21 with the 151,492 electors, it appears that $\frac{1}{40}$ of them, or $\frac{1}{160}$ of the entire population, have the power of passing all the laws in your Honorable House.

" And your petitioners further find, on investigation, that this majority of 331 members are composed of 163 Tories or Conservatives, 134 Whigs and Liberals, and only 34 who call themselves Radicals; and out of this limited number it is questionable whether 10 can be found who are truly the representatives of the wants and wishes of the producing classes.

" Your petitioners also find that 15 members of your Honorable House are returned by electors under 200; 55 under 300; 99 under 400; 121 under 500; 150 under 600; 196 under 700; 214 under 800; 240 under 900; and 256 under 1,000; and that many of these constituencies are divided between two members.

" They also find that your Honorable House, which is said to be exclusively the people's or the Commons' House, contains *two hundred and five persons who are immediately or remotely related to the Peers of the Realm.*

" Also that your Honorable House contains 1 marquess, 7 earls, 19 viscounts, 32 lords, 25 right honorables, 52 honorables, 63 baronets, 13 knights, 3 admirals, 7 lord-lieutenants, 42 deputy and vice-lieutenants, 1 general, 5 lieutenant-generals, 9 major-generals, 32 colonels, 33 lieutenant-colonels, 10 majors, 49 captains in army and navy, 10 lieutenants, 2 cornets, 58 barristers, 3 solicitors, 40 bankers, 33 East India proprietors, 13 West India proprietors, 52 place-men, 114 patrons of church livings having the patronage of 274 livings between them; the names of whom your petitioners can furnish at the request of your Honorable House.

"Your petitioners therefore respectfully submit to your Honorable House that these facts afford abundant proofs that you do not represent the numbers or the interests of the millions; but that the persons composing it have interests for the most part foreign or directly opposed to the true interests of the great body of the people.

" That perceiving the tremendous power you possess over the lives, liberty and labor of the unrepresented millions—perceiving the *military* and *civil forces* at your command—the *revenue* at your disposal—the *relief* of the poor in your hands —the *public press* in your power, by enactments expressly excluding the working classes alone — moreover, the power of delegating to others the whole control of the *monetary arrangements* of the Kingdom, by which the laboring classes may be silently plundered or suddenly suspended from employment—seeing all these elements of power wielded by your Honorable

House as at present constituted, and fearing the consequences that may result if a thorough reform is not speedily had recourse to, your petitioners earnestly pray your Honorable House *to enact the following as the law of these realms*, with such other essential details as your Honorable House shall deem necessary:—

"A LAW FOR EQUALLY REPRESENTING THE PEOPLE OF GREAT
BRITAIN AND IRELAND.

EQUAL REPRESENTATION

"That the United Kingdom be divided into 200 electoral districts; dividing, as nearly as possible, an equal number of inhabitants; and that each district do send a representative to Parliament.

UNIVERSAL SUFFRAGE

"That every person producing proof of his being 21 years of age, to the clerk of the parish in which he has resided six months, shall be entitled to have his name registered as a voter. That the time for registering in each year be from the 1st of January to the 1st of March.

ANNUAL PARLIAMENTS

"That a general election do take place on the 24th of June in each year, and that each vacancy be filled up a fortnight after it occurs. That the hours for voting be from six o'clock in the morning till six o'clock in the evening.

NO PROPERTY QUALIFICATIONS

"That there shall be no property qualifications for members; but on a requisition, signed by 200 voters, in favor of any candidate being presented to the clerk of the parish in which they reside, such candidate shall be put in nomination. And the list of all the candidates nominated throughout the district shall be stuck on the church door in every parish, to enable voters to judge of their qualification.

VOTE BY BALLOT

" That each voter must vote in the parish in which he resides. That each parish provide as many balloting boxes as there are candidates proposed in the district; and that a temporary place be fitted up in each parish church for the purpose of *secret voting*. And, on the day of election, as each voter passes orderly on to the ballot, he shall have given to him, by the officer in attendance, a balloting ball, which he shall drop into the box of his favorite candidate. At the close of the day the votes shall be counted, by the proper officers, and the numbers stuck on the church doors. The following day the clerk of the district and two examiners shall collect the votes of all the parishes throughout the district, and cause the name of the successful candidate to be posted in every parish of the district.

SITTINGS AND PAYMENTS TO MEMBERS

" That the members do take their seats in Parliament on the first Monday in October next after their election, and continue their sittings every day (Sundays excepted) till the business of the sitting is terminated, but not later than the 1st of September. They shall meet every day (during the Session) for business at 10 o'clock in the morning, and adjourn at 4. And every member shall be paid quarterly out of the public treasury £400 a year. That all electoral officers shall be elected by universal suffrage.

" By passing the foregoing as the law of the land, you will confer a great blessing on the people of England; and your petitioners, as in duty bound, will ever pray."

APPENDIX B

The People's Charter

Being a bill to provide for the just representation of the people of Great Britain and Ireland in the Commons' House of Parliament. (Published on the 8th of May, 1838).

WHEREAS to insure, as far as it is possible by human forethought and wisdom, the just government of the people, it is necessary to subject those who have the power of making the laws to a wholesome and strict responsibility to those whose duty it is to obey them when made;

And, whereas, this responsibility is best enforced through the instrumentality of a body which emanates directly from, and is itself immediately subject to, the whole people, and which completely represents their feelings and their interests.

And, whereas, the Commons' House of Parliament now exercises, in the name and on the supposed behalf of the people, the power of making the laws, it ought, in order to fulfill with wisdom and with honesty the great duties imposed on it, to be made the faithful and accurate representation of the people's wishes, feelings, and interests.

Be it therefore enacted:

That, from and after the passing of this Act, every male inhabitant of these realms be entitled to vote for the election of a member of Parliament; subject, however, to the following conditions:

1. That he be a native of these realms, or a foreigner who has lived in this country upward of two years, and been naturalized.

2. That he be twenty-one years of age.

3. That he be not proved insane when the lists of voters are revised.

4. That he be not convicted of felony within six months from and after the passing of this Act.[1]

5. That his electoral rights be not suspended for bribery at election, or for personation, or for forgery of election certificates, according to the penalties of this Act.

ELECTORAL DISTRICTS

I. Be it enacted that for the purpose of obtaining an equal representation of the people in the Commons' House of Parliament, the United Kingdom be divided into 300 electoral districts.[2]

II. That each such district contain, as nearly as may be, an equal number of inhabitants.

III. That the number of inhabitants be taken from the last census, and as soon as possible after the next ensuing decennial census shall have been taken, the electoral districts be made to conform thereto.

IV. That each electoral district be named after the principal city or borough within its limits.

V. That each electoral district return one representative to sit in the Commons' House of Parliament.

VI. That the Secretary of State for the Home Department shall appoint three competent persons as commissioners, and as many sub-commissioners as may be necessary for settling the boundaries of each of the 300 electoral districts, and so on from time to time, whenever a new decennial census of the people be taken.

VII. That the necessary expenses of the said commissioners,

---

[1] " The People's Charter," as revised at a conference held at Birmingham, December, 1842, reads: " 4. That he be not undergoing the sentence of the laws at the time when called upon to exercise the electoral right."

[2] There are, say, 6,000,000 of men eligible to vote. This number, divided by 300, gives 20,000 to each member.

sub-commissioners, clerks, and other persons employed by them in the performance of their duties, be paid out of the public treasury.

REGISTRATION OFFICERS

Be it enacted, that for the purpose of procuring an accurate registration of voters, for finally adjudicating in all cases of objections made against persons claiming to be registered, for receiving the nominations of Members of Parliament and Returning Officers, and declaring their election; as well as for conducting and superintending all matters connected with registration, nomination, and election, according to the provisions of this Act, the following officers be appointed:

1. Returning Officers for each electorial district.
2. Deputy-Returning Officers for each district.
3. A Registration Clerk for every parish containing
number of inhabitants, or for every two or more parishes, if united for the purpose of this Act.

RETURNING OFFICER, AND HIS DUTIES

I. Be it enacted, that at the first general election after the passing of this Act, a returning officer be elected for every electoral district throughout the kingdom, and so in like manner at the end of every three years.[1]

II. That, at the end of every such period, the returning officer for each district be nominated in like manner, and elected at the same time, as the Member of Parliament for the district; he shall be eligible to be re-elected.

III. That vacancies occasioned by the death, removal, or resignation of the returning officer, shall in like manner be filled up as vacancies for Members of Parliament, for the unexpired term of the three years.[2]

IV. That every returning officer shall appoint a deputy re-

[1] The revised "Charter" reads: "at the end of every year."

[2] The revised "Charter" reads: "for the unexpired term of the year."

turning officer, for the day of election, for every balloting place within his district, and in all cases be responsible for the just fulfilment of the duties of such deputies.

V. That it be the duty of the returning officers to appoint a registration clerk for every parish within his district containing   number of inhabitants, or for every two or more parishes if united for the purposes of this Act; and that in all cases he be responsible for the just fulfilment of the duties of such clerks.

VI. That he also see that proper balloting places, and such other erections as may be necessary, be provided by each parish (or any number that may be united) and that the balloting boxes be made and provided according to the provisions of this Act.

VII. That he receive the lists of voters from all the parishes in his district, in which lists shall be marked or specified the names of the persons who have been objected to by the registration clerks or any other persons.

VIII. That between the first of April and the first of May in each year, he shall hold *open* courts of adjudication at such a number of places within his district as he may deem necessary, of which courts (place and time of meeting) he shall cause due notice to be given in each parish of the district, and at the same time invite all persons who have made objections, and who have been objected to. And, after hearing the statements that may be made by both parties, he shall *finally adjudicate* whether the voters' names be placed on the register or not.

IX. That the returning officer shall then cause to be made out alphabetical lists of all the registered voters in all the parishes within his district; which lists, signed and attested by himself, shall be used at all elections for the district. Such lists to be sold to the public at reasonably low prices.

X. That the returning officer receive all nominations for the member of his district, as well as for the returning officer of his district, and shall give public notice of the same according to the provisions of this Act; he shall also receive from the

Speaker of the House of Commons the orders for any new election, in case of the death or resignation of the member of the district, as well as the orders to superintend and conduct the election of any other district, in case of the death or resignation of the returning officer of such district.

XI. That the returning officer shall also receive the returns from all the parishes within his district, on the day of election; and on the day following the election he shall proclaim the state of the ballot, as directed by this Act, and perform the several duties appertaining to his office, as herein made and provided.

XII. That the returning officer be paid for fulfilling the duties of his office, the sum of   per annum, as hereinafter mentioned.

XIII. That, upon a petition being presented to the House of Commons by at least one hundred qualified electors, against any returning officer,[1] complaining of corruption in the exercise of his office, or of incapacity, such complaints shall be inquired into by a committee of the House, consisting of seven members; and, on their report being read, the members present shall then determine whether such returning officer be or be not guilty, or be or be not incapacitated.

XIV. That, for conducting the first elections after the passing of this Act, a returning officer for each district be temporarily appointed by the Secretary of State, to perform the duties prescribed by this Act. He shall resign his office as soon as the new one is appointed, and be paid as hereinafter mentioned.—*See Penalties.*

DEPUTY RETURNING OFFICER, AND HIS DUTIES

I. Be it enacted, that a deputy returning officer be appointed by the district returning officer to preside at each balloting place on the day of election, such deputy to be subject and responsible to his authority, as well as to the provisions of this Act.

---

[1] The revised "Charter" reads: "at least one hundred qualified electors of the district, against any returning officer of the same."

II. That it be the duty of the deputy returning officer to provide a number of competent persons, not exceeding   , to aid him in taking the ballot, and for performing the necessary business thereof.

III. That the deputy returning officer shall see that proper registration lists are provided, and that the ballot begin at six o'clock in the morning precisely, and end at six o'clock in the afternoon of the same day.

IV. That the deputy returning officer, in the presence of the agents of the candidates, examine and seal the balloting-boxes previous to the commencement of the balloting; he shall, in like manner, declare the number of votes for each candidate, and shall cause a copy, signed by himself, to be forwarded to the returning officer of the district, and another copy to the registration clerk of the parish.

V. That the deputy returning officer be paid for his services as hereinafter mentioned.—*See Penalties.*

THE REGISTRATION CLERK, HIS DUTIES

I. Be it enacted, that a registration clerk be appointed by the district returning officer for every parish within his district containing   inhabitants; or for every two or more parishes that may be united for the purposes of this Act; such clerk to be responsible to his authority, as well as to the provisions of this Act.

II. That for the purpose of obtaining a correct registration of all the voters in each electoral district, the registration clerk of every parish, as aforesaid, throughout the kingdom, shall, on or before the 1st of February in each year, take or cause to be taken round to every dwelling house [1] in his parish, a printed notice of the following form:

Mr. John Jones, you are hereby required, within six days from the date hereof, to fill up this list with the names of all male inhabitants of your house, of 21 years of age, and upwards; stating their respec-

[1] The revised "Charter" reads: "to every dwelling-house, poor-house, or union-workhouse in his parish."

tive ages, and the time they have resided with you; or, in neglect thereof, to forfeit the sum of one pound.[1]

A. B., *Registration Clerk.*

NAME.	ADDRESS.	AGE.	TIME OF RESIDENCE.
JOHN JONES.	6 Upper North Place.	21 years.	3 months.

N. B.—This list will be called for at the expiration of six days from this date.

III. That, at the expiration of six days, as aforesaid, the registration clerk shall collect, or cause to be collected, the aforesaid lists, and shall cause to be made out from them an alphabetical list of all persons who are of the proper age and residence to qualify them as voters, according to the provisions of this Act.

IV. That if the registration clerk shall have any just reason to believe that the names, ages, or time of residence of any persons inserted in the aforesaid list are falsely entered, or not in accordance with the provisions of this Act, he shall write the words " objected to " opposite such names; and so in like manner against the names of every person he may have just reason to consider ineligible, according to the provisions of this Act.

V. That on or before the 8th of March in each year, the registration clerk shall cause the aforesaid alphabetical list of voters to be stuck against all church and chapel doors, market-houses, town-halls, session-houses,[2] and such other conspicuous places as he may deem necessary, from the 8th of March till the 22nd. He shall also cause a copy of such list to lie at his office, to be perused by any person without a fee, at all

---

[1] The revised "Charter" reads: "the sum of one pound for every name omitted."

[2] The revised "Charter" added: "poor houses, union workhouses."

reasonable hours; and copies of the said list shall be sold to the public at a reasonably low price.

VI. That, on or before the 25th of March, the registration clerk shall take, or cause to be taken a copy of the aforesaid list of voters to the returning officer of his district, which list shall be signed by himself, and be presented as a just and impartial list, according to his judgment, of all persons within his parish who are eligible according to their claims, as well as of all those who have been objected to by himself or other persons.

VII. That the registration clerk shall attend the court of adjudication, according to the notice he shall receive from the returning officer, to revise his list, and shall perform all the duties of his office as herein provided.

VIII. That the registration clerk be paid for his services in the manner hereinafter mentioned.

ARRANGEMENT FOR REGISTRATION

I. Be it enacted, that every householder, as well as every person occupying or having charge of a dwelling-house,[1] who shall receive a notice from the registration clerk as aforesaid, shall cause the said notice to be correctly filled up with the names, ages, and time of residence of every male inmate or inhabitant of his or her house, of twenty-one years of age and upwards, within six days of the day of the date of such notice, and shall carefully preserve the same till it is called for by the registration clerk, or his proper officer.

II. That when the list of voters is made out from these notices, and stuck on the church doors,[2] as aforesaid, any person who finds his name not inserted in the list, and who believes he is duly qualified as a voter, shall, on presenting to the registration clerk a notice in the following form, have his name added to the list of voters:

[1] The revised "Charter" reads: "poor house, or union workhouse".
[2] The revised "Charter" added: "and places."

I, John Jones, carpenter, residing at   in the district of
being twenty one years of age, and having resided at the above place
during the last three months, require to be placed on the list of voters,
as a qualified elector for the said district.

III. That any person who is qualified as a voter in any
electoral district, and shall have removed to any other parish
within the said district, on presenting to the registration clerk
of the parish he then resides in, his voter's certificate as proof
of this, or the written testimony of any registration clerk who
has previously registered him, he shall be entitled to be placed
on the list of voters as aforesaid.

IV. That if an elector of any parish in the district have any
just grounds for believing that any person disqualified by this
Act has been put upon any parish register within the said
district, he may, at any reasonable hour, between the 1st and
the 20th day of March, cause the following notices to be delivered; the one at the residence of the registration clerk, and
the other at the residence of the person objected to; and the
registration clerk shall, in like manner, send notice of the
ground of objection to all persons he may object to, as aforesaid:

To the Registration Clerk.

I, William Smith, elector of the parish of   in the district
of   object to A. B. being on the register of voters, believing
him to be disqualified.
                    Dated this day, *etc.*

To the person objected to:

Mr. A. B. of   I, William Smith, elector of the parish
of   in the district of   object to your name being
on the register of voters for the following reasons:—(here state the
reasons)—and I will support my objections by proofs before the Returning Officer of the District.
                    Dated this day, *etc.*

V. That if the person thus objecting neglect to attend the
court of the returning officer at the proper time, to state his

objections, he shall be fined ten shillings for every such neglect, the same to be levied on his goods and chattels, provided he is not prevented from attending by sickness or accident, in which case his medical certificate, or a certificate signed by ten voters certifying such fact, shall be forwarded to the returning officer, who shall then determine whether the claim to be put on the register be allowed or not.

VI. That if the person objected to fails to attend the court of the returning officer at the proper time, to substantiate his claim, his name shall be erased from the register, provided he is not prevented by sickness or accident; in which case a certificate shall be forwarded, and the returning officer shall determine, as before directed.

VII. That if it should be proved before the returning officer, in his open court of adjudication, that any person has frivolously or vexatiously objected to any one being placed on the list of voters, such person objecting shall be fined twenty shillings, the same to be levied on his goods and chattels.[1]

VIII. That, as early as possible after the lists are revised as aforesaid, the returning officer shall cause a copy of the same to be forwarded to every registration clerk within his district.

IX. That the registration clerk of every parish shall then correctly copy from such lists the name, age, and residence of every qualified elector within his parish or parishes, into a book made for that purpose, and shall place a number opposite each name. He shall then, within   days, take, or cause to be taken, to all such electors, *a voter's certificate* of the following form, the number on which shall correspond with the number in the aforesaid book:

No. 123. This is to certify that James Jones, of   is eligible to vote for one person to be returned to Parliament (as well as for the Returning Officer) for the district of   for one year from the date hereof.

Dated

Registration Clerk.

[1] The revised "Charter" provides for a fine of "twenty shillings and expenses, the same to be levied on his goods and chattels, and paid to the person objected to."

X. That if any person lose his voter's certificate by fire, or any other accident, he shall not have a new certificate till the next registration; but on the day of any election, if he can establish his identity, on the testimony of two witnesses, to the satisfaction of the registration clerk, as being the qualified voter described in the registration book, he shall be allowed to vote.

XI. That the returning officer is hereby authorized and commanded to attach any small parishes *to any adjacent parish* [1] within his district for the purposes of this Act, and not otherwise; and in like manner to unite all extra-parochial places to some adjacent parish.—*See Penalties.*

ARRANGEMENT FOR NOMINATIONS

I. Be it enacted, that for the purpose of guarding against too great a number, who might otherwise be heedlessly proposed, as well as for giving time for the electors to inquire into the merits of the persons who may be nominated for members of Parliament, as well as for returning officers, that all nominations be taken as hereinafter directed.

II. That for all general elections of members of Parliament a requisition of the following form, signed by at least one hundred qualified electors of the district, be delivered to the returning officer of the district, between the 1st and 10th day of May in each year; and that such requisition constitute the nomination of such person as a candidate for the district:

We, the undersigned electors of the district of   recommend A. B. of   as a fit and proper person to represent the people of this district in the Commons' House of Parliament, the said A. B. being a qualified elector of these realms.[2]

Dated, *etc.*

Signed.

III. That the returning officer of every electoral district

---

[1] The italicized phrase was omitted in the revised "Charter."

[2] The revised "Charter" reads: "the said A. B. being qualified to be an elector according to the provisions of this Act.

shall, on or before the 13th of May in each year, cause a list
of all the candidates thus nominated to be stuck up against all
church and chapel doors, market-houses, town-halls, session-
houses,[1] and such other conspicuous places within the district
as he may deem necessary.

IV. That whenever a vacancy is occasioned in any district
by the death, resignation, or other cause, of the member of
Parliament, the returning officer of that district shall, within
three days after the receipt of his orders from the Speaker
of the House of Commons, give notice thereof in all the
parishes of his district in the manner described for giving
notices, and he shall at the same time request all nominations
to be made as aforesaid, within ten days from the receipt of his
order, and shall also appoint the day of election within eighteen
days from the receipt of such order from the Speaker of the
House of Commons.

V. That if, from any circumstances, no person has been
nominated as a candidate for the district on or before the 10th
of May, persons may then be nominated in the manner described as aforesaid at any time previous to the 20th of May,
but not otherwise.[2]

VI. That at the first election after the passing of this Act,
and at the expiration of every three succeeding years, the
nomination of candidates for the returning officer be made in
the same manner as for the members of Parliament, and
nominations for vacancies that may occur in like manner.

VII. That if two or more persons are nominated as aforesaid for members to serve in Parliament for the district, the
returning officer shall, at any time between the 15th and 31st
of May, (Sundays excepted), appoint such times and places
(not exceeding   ) as he shall think most convenient
to the electors of the district for the candidates to appear be-

---

[1] In the revised "Charter," "poor-houses, and union workhouses"
were added.

[2] The revised "Charter" reads: "but not after that date."

[3] The revised "Charter" reads: "at the expiration of every year."

fore them, then and there to explain their views and solicit the suffrages of the electors.

VIII. That the returning officer see that the places above described be convenient for the purpose, and that as many such erections be put up as may be necessary; the same to be paid for by the returning officer, and charged in his account as hereinafter mentioned.

IX. That for the purpose of keeping good order and public decorum, the returning officer either take the chair at such meeting himself, or appoint a deputy for that purpose.

X. That, provided only one candidate be proposed for a member of Parliament for the district by the time herein before mentioned, the returning officer cause notice to be given, as hereinafter mentioned, that such candidate is elected a member for the district; and if only one candidate be proposed for the returning officer, he shall in like manner be declared duly elected.

XI. That no other qualification shall be required for members to serve in the Commons' House of Parliament, than the choice of the electors.[1]—*See Penalties.*

ARRANGEMENT FOR ELECTIONS

I. Be it enacted, that a general election of members of Parliament, for the electoral districts of the United Kingdom, take place on the first Monday in June in each year; and that all vacancies, by death or otherwise, shall be filled up as nearly as possible within eighteen days after they occur.

II. That a general election of returning officer for all the districts take place at the expiration of every three years on the first Monday in June, and at the same time members of

---

[1] The revised "Charter" provides: " XI. That no other qualification shall be required than the choice of the electors, according to the provisions of this Act; providing that no persons, excepting the cabinet ministers, be eligible to serve in the Commons' House of Parliament who are in the receipt of any emolument derivable from any place or places held under Government, or of retired allowances arising therefrom."

Parliament are to be elected; and that all vacancies be filled up, as nearly as possible, within eighteen days after they occur.

III. That every person who has been registered as aforesaid, and who has a voter's certificate, shall have the right of voting in the district in which he has been registered, and in that only, and of voting for the member of Parliament for that district, and the returning officer for the district, and for those only.

IV. That, for the purpose of taking the votes of the qualified electors, the parish officer in every parish of the district (or in every two parishes if united for that purpose) shall cause proper places to be privided, so as to admit of the arrangements described in Schedule A, and so constructed (either permanently or temporarily as they may think proper) that the votes may be taken with due despatch, and so as to secure the elector while voting from being inspected by any other person.

V. That the parish officers of every parish in the district provide a sufficient number of balloting-boxes, made after a model described in Schedule B (or made on one plan by persons appointed to make them, as was the case with weights and measures), and none but such boxes, duly certified, shall be used.

VI. That immediately preceeding the commencement of the balloting, each ballot-box shall be opened by the deputy returning officer (or otherwise examined, as the case may be), in the presence of an agent appointed by each candidate, and shall then be sealed by him and by the agents of the candidates, and not again be opened until the balloting has finally closed, when notice shall be given to such of the agents of the candidates as may then be present to attend to the opening of the boxes and ascertaining the number of votes for each candidate.

VII. That the deputy returning officer preside in the front of the ballot-box, and see that the balloting is conducted with strict impartiality and justice; and that the various clerks, assistants, and parish constables properly perform their respective duties, and that strict order and decorum be preserved among the friends of the candidates, as well as among all persons employed in conducting the election; and he is hereby authorized and empowered to cause all persons to be taken into custody who interrupt the proceedings of the election, seek to contravene the provisions of this Act, or fail to obey his lawful authority.

VIII. That during the time the balloting is going on, two agents of each candidate may be in the space fronting the ballot-box, and immediately behind the deputy returning officer, in order that they may see that the election is fairly conducted; such persons to be provided by the deputy returning officer with cards of admission, and to pass in and out by the entrance assigned them.

IX. That the registration clerk of every parish in the district, who has been appointed for the purposes of registration, be at the balloting place, in the station assigned him, previously to the commencement of the balloting, and see that no person pass on to the balloting place till he has examined his certificate and seen that it corresponds with the registration list.

X. That the parish constables and the officers stationed at the entrance of the balloting place, shall not permit any person to enter unless he shows his voter's certificate, except the persons employed in conducting the election, or those persons who have proved the loss of their voter's certificate.

XI. That at the end of every three years,[1] or whenever the returning officer is elected at the same time as the member for the district, a division shall be made in the balloting places, and the boxes and balloting so arranged as to ensure the candidates the strictest impartiality and justice, by preventing the voter from giving two votes for either of the candidates.

XII. That on the day of election, the balloting commence at six o'clock in the forenoon and terminate at six o'clock in the afternoon of the same day.

XIII. That when any voter's certificate is examined by the registration clerk, and found to be correct, he shall be allowed to pass on to the next barrier, where a balloting-ball shall be

[1] The revised "Charter" reads: "at the end of every year."

given him by the person appointed for that purpose; he shall
then pass on to the balloting box, and, with all due despatch,
shall put the balloting-ball into the aperture opposite the name [1]
of the candidate he wishes to vote for, after which he shall,
without delay, leave the room by the door assigned for the
purpose.

XIV. That, at the close of the balloting, the deputy returning officer, in the presence of the agents of the candidates and
other persons present, shall break open the seals of the balloting-boxes, and ascertain the number for each candidate; he
shall then cause copies of the same to be publicly posted outside
the balloting place; and immediately forward (by a trusty
messenger) a copy of the same, signed by himself and the
agents present, to the returning officer of the district; he shall
then deliver a similar copy to the registration clerk, who shall
carefully preserve the same, and produce it if necessary.

XV. That the persons employed as assistants, for inspecting
the certificates and attending on the balloting, be paid as hereinafter mentioned.

XVI. That all the expense of registration, nominations and
election, as aforesaid, together with the salaries of the returning officers, registration clerk, assistants, constables, and such
other persons as may be necessary, as well as the expense of
all balloting places, balloting-boxes, hustings, and other necessaries for the purposes of this Act, be paid out of an equitable
district rate, which a District Board, composed of one parochial
officer chosen by each of the parishes in the district, or for any
two or more parishes, if united for the purposes of this Act, are
hereby empowered and commanded to levy on all householders
within the district.

XVIII. That all expenses necessary for the purposes of this
Act incurred within the district be paid by the District Board
as aforesaid, or their treasurer; that the salaries of all officers
and assistants required for the purposes of this Act, be fixed

[1] The revised "Charter" reads "into the box of the candidate."

and paid by the said Board, according to the expenses and duties of the various localities.[1]

XVIII. That all accounts of receipts and expenditure for electoral purposes shall be kept distinct, and be audited by auditors appointed by the District Board, as aforesaid; copies of which accounts shall be printed for the use of the respective parishes in the district.

XIX. That all canvassing for members of Parliament, as well as for returning officers, is hereby declared to be illegal, and meetings for that purpose during the balloting, on the day of election, are hereby also declared to be illegal.—*See Penalties.*

DURATION OF PARLIAMENT

I. Be it enacted, that the Members of the House of Commons, chosen as aforesaid, shall meet on the first Monday in June in each year, and continue their sittings from time to time as they may deem it convenient, till the first Monday in June following, when the next new Parliament shall be chosen; they shall be eligible to be re-elected.

II. That during an adjournment they be liable to be called together by the executive in cases of emergency.

III. That a register be kept of the daily attendance of each member, which, at the close of the session, shall be printed as a sessional paper, showing how the members have attended.

PAYMENT OF MEMBERS

I. Be it enacted, that every member of the House of Commons, be entitled, at the close of the session, to a writ of ex-

---

[1] The Committee having considered that, as the duties and expenses of all these various offices will greatly vary, according to their localities, it will be unwise to have a sum fixed by Parliament and paid out of the treasury. Believing, moreover, that a just system of representation will soon purify the local corruptions that exist, they think that the united expenditure will be much less under the immediate superintendence of the local authorities, when responsible to the people, than under the management of government and their subordiate agents.

penses on the Treasury, for his legislative duties in the public service, and shall be paid £500 [1] per annum.[2]

PENALTIES

I. Be it enacted, that if any person cause himself to be registered in more than one electoral district, and vote in more than one such district, upon conviction thereof before any two justices of the peace within either of such districts, he shall incur for the first offence the penalty of three months' imprisonment, and for the second offence twelve months' imprisonment.

II. That any person who shall be convicted as aforesaid of wilfully neglecting to fill up his or her notice within the proper time, or of leaving out the name of any inmate in his or her notice, shall for the first offence incur the penalty of five pounds, and three months' imprisonment for the second offence.[3]

III. That any person who shall be convicted as aforesaid of forging any name, age, or time of residence on any notice, shall for the first offence incur the penalty of three months' imprisonment, and for the second offence be deprived of his elective rights for five years.[4]

IV. That any person who shall be convicted as aforesaid, of having in any manner obtained the certificate of an elector

[1] The amount was omitted in the revised "Charter."

[2] The Committee understand that the *daily* payment of members of Parliament has operated beneficially in Canada; but they fear that such mode of payment holds out a motive for lengthening the sessions unnecessarily; and if the time of sitting is limited by law, it may lead to too hasty legislation, both of which evils are obviated by an annual payment.

[3] The revised "Charter" reads: "the penalty of one pound for every name omitted, and for the second offence, incur the penalty of three months' imprisonment, and be deprived of his electoral rights for three years."

[4] The revised "Charter" reads: "and for the second offence three months' imprisonment and be deprived of his elective rights for three years."

other than his own, and of having voted or attempted to vote by means of such false certificate, shall for the first offence incur the penalty of six months' imprisonment, and for the second offence six months' imprisonment, and be deprived of his elective rights for five years.[1]

V. That any person who shall be convicted, as aforesaid, of having forged a voter's certificate, or of having forged the name of any person to any certificate; or having voted or attempted to vote on such forged certificate; knowing such to have been forged, shall for the first offence incur the penalty of twelve months' imprisonment, and for the second offence twelve months' imprisonment, and be deprived of his elective rights for five years.[2]

VI. That any person who shall be convicted as aforesaid, of having forged, or caused to be forged, the names of any voters to a requisition nominating a member of Parliament or a returning officer, shall for the first offence incur the penalty of three months' imprisonment, and twelve months for the second offence.[3]

VII. That any person who shall be convicted as aforesaid of bribery, in order to secure his election, shall be subject for the first offence to incur the penalty of two years' imprisonment, and for the second offence shall be imprisoned two years, and be deprived of his elective rights for five years.

VIII. That any agent of any candidate, or any other person, who shall be convicted, as aforesaid, of bribery at any election, shall be subject for the first offence to incur the penalty of twelve months' imprisonment, and for the second

[1] The revised "Charter" fixes a penalty of three months for the first offence, and three months' imprisonment and the loss of elective rights for three years for the second offence.

[2] In the revised "Charter" the term of imprisonment in both cases is reduced to three months, and the loss of elective rights to three years.

[3] The revised "Charter" reads: "and for the second offence three months' imprisonment, and to be deprived of his elective rights for three years."

offence twelve months' imprisonment, and be deprived of his elective rights for five years.

IX. That any person who shall be convicted, as aforesaid, of going from house to house, or place to place, to solicit in any way votes in favor of any member of Parliament [1] or returning officer, after the nomination as aforesaid, shall for the first offence incur the penalty of one month's imprisonment, and for the second offence two months'.

X. That any person who shall be convicted as aforesaid of calling together, or causing an election meeting to be held in any district during the day of election, shall for the first offence incur the penalty of three months' imprisonment, and for the second offence six months.

XI. That any person who shall be convicted, as aforesaid, of interrupting the balloting, or the business of the election, shall incur the penalty of three months' imprisonment for the first offence, and six months' for the second.

XII. That if any messenger, who may be sent with the state of the ballot to the returning officer, or with any other notice, shall wilfully delay the same, or in any way by his consent or conduct cause the same to be delayed, on conviction as aforesaid, shall incur the penalty of six months' imprisonment.

XIII. That any returning officer who shall be convicted, as aforesaid, of having neglected to appoint proper officers as directed by this Act, to see that proper balloting places and balloting boxes are provided, and to give the notices and perform the duties herein required of him, shall forfeit for each such neglect the sum of £20.

XIV. That if any returning officer be found gulty *by the House of Commons* of bribery or corrupt practices in the execution *of any* of the duties herein assigned to him, he shall incur the penalty of twelve months' imprisonment, and be deprived of his elective rights for five years.[2]

[1] The revised "Charter" reads: "in favor of any candidate for Parliament."

[2] The italicized words were omitted in the revised "Charter."

XV. That if any deputy returning officer be convicted, as aforesaid, of having neglected to perform any of the duties herein assigned him, he shall forfeit for such neglect three pounds.

XVI. That if any deputy returning officer be convicted, as aforesaid, of bribery or corrupt practices in the execution of the duties of his office, he shall incur the penalty of six months' imprisonment, and the deprivation of his elective rights for five years.[1]

XVII. That if any registration clerk be convicted, as aforesaid, of having neglected to perform any of the duties herein assigned him, he shall forfeit for each such neglect five pounds.

XVIII. That if any registration clerk be convicted, as aforesaid, of bribery or corrupt practices in the execution of the duties of his office, he shall incur the penalty of six months' imprisonment, and the deprivation of his elective rights for five years.[2]

XIX. That if the parochial officers in any parish neglect or refuse to comply with any of the provisions of this Act, they shall forfeit for every such neglect the sum of £50.[3]

XX. That all fines and penalties incurred under the provisions of this Act, be recoverable before any two justices of the peace, within the district where the offence shall have been committed, and in default of payment, the said justices shall issue their warrant of distress against the goods and chattels of the offender; or in default of sufficient distress, he shall be imprisoned three months.[4]

N. B.—All Acts and parts of Acts relating to registration, nominations, or elections, as well as duration of Parliament and sittings of members, must be repealed.[5]

---

[1] The revised "Charter" reads: "three years."

[2] The revised "Charter" provides for deprivation of rights for three years.

[3] The revised "Charter" reads: "or, in default of payment, twelve months' imprisonment."

[4] The revised "Charter" reads: "shall be imprisoned according to the provisions of this Act."

[5] The revised "Charter" reads: "are hereby repealed."

APPENDIX C

" NATIONAL PETITION

*" Unto the Honorable the Commons of the United Kingdom
of Great Britain and Ireland in Parliament assembled, the
Petition of the undersigned, their suffering countrymen,*

" HUMBLY SHEWETH,

" That we, your petitioners, dwell in a land whose merchants
are noted for enterprise, whose manufacturers are very skil-
ful, and whose workmen are proverbial for their industry.

" The land itself is goodly, the soil rich, and the temperature
wholesome; it is abundantly furnished with the materials of
commerce and trade; it has numerous and convenient harbors;
in facility of internal communication it exceeds all others.

" For three-and-twenty years we have enjoyed a profound
peace.

" Yet, with all these elements of national prosperity, and
with every disposition and capacity to take advantage of
them, we find ourselves overwhelmed with public and private
suffering.

" We are bowed down under a load of taxes; which, notwithstanding, fall greatly short of the wants of our rulers;
our traders are trembling on the verge of bankruptcy; our
workmen are starving; capital brings no profit, and labor no
remuneration; the home of the artificer is desolate, and the
warehouse of the pawnbroker is full; the workhouse is
crowded, and the manufactory is deserted.

" We have looked on every side, we have searched diligently
in order to find out the causes of a distress so sore and so
long continued.

" We can discover none in nature, or in Providence.

" Heaven has dealt graciously by the people; but the fool-
ishness of our rulers has made the goodness of God of none
effect.

" The energies of a mighty kingdom have been wasted in
building up the power of selfish and ignorant men, and its
resources squandered for their aggrandisement.

" The good of a party has been advanced to the sacrifice of
the good of the nation; the few have governed for the interest
of the few, while the interest of the many has been neglected,
or insolently and tyrannously trampled upon.

" It was the fond expectation of the people that a remedy
for the greater part, if not for the whole, of their grievances,
would be found in the Reform Act of 1832.

" They were taught to regard that Act as a wise means to
a worthy end; as the machinery of an improved legislation,
when the will of the masses would be at length potential.

" They have been bitterly and basely deceived.

" The fruit which looked so fair to the eye has turned to
dust and ashes when gathered.

" The Reform Act has effected a transfer of power from
one domineering faction to another, and left the people as
helpless as before.

" Our slavery has been exchanged for an apprenticeship to
liberty, which has aggravated the painful feeling of our social
degradation, by adding to it the sickening of still deferred hope.

" We come before your Honorable House to tell you, with
all humility, that this state of things must not be permitted to
continue; that it cannot long continue without very seriously
endangering the stability of the throne and the peace of the
kingdom; and that if by God's help and all lawful and constitutional appliances an end can be put to it, we are fully resolved that it shall speedily come to an end.

" We tell your Honorable House that the capital of the
master must no longer be deprived of its due reward; that
the laws which make food dear, and those which by making
money scarce, make labor cheap, must be abolished; that taxation must be made to fall on property, not on industry; that

the good of the many, as it is the only legitimate end, so must it be the sole study of the Government.

"As a preliminary essential to these and other requisite changes; as means by which alone the interests of the people can be effectually vindicated and secured, we demand that those interests be confided to the keeping of the people.

"When the state calls for defenders, when it calls for money, no consideration of poverty or ignorance can be pleaded in refusal or delay of the call.

"Required as we are, universally, to support and obey the laws, nature and reason entitle us to demand that in the making of the laws, the universal voice should be implicitly listened to.

"We perform the duties of freemen; we must have the privileges of freemen.

"WE DEMAND UNIVERSAL SUFFRAGE.

"The suffrage, to be exempt from the corruption of the wealthy and the violence of the powerful, must be secret.

"The assertion of our right necessarily involves the power of its uncontrolled exercise.

"WE DEMAND THE BALLOT.

"The connection between the representatives and the people, to be beneficial, must be intimate.

"The legislative and constituent powers, for correction and for instruction, ought to be brought into frequent contact.

"Errors which are comparatively light when susceptible of a speedy popular remedy, may produce the most disastrous effects when permitted to grow inveterate through years of compulsory endurance.

"To public safety as well as public confidence, frequent elections are essential.

"WE DEMAND ANNUAL PARLIAMENTS.

"With power to choose, and freedom in choosing, the range of our choice must be unrestricted.

"We are compelled, by the existing laws, to take for our representatives men who are incapable of appreciating our difficulties, or who have little sympathy with them; merchants who have retired from trade, and no longer feel its harassings; proprietors of land who are alike ignorant of its evils and their cure; lawyers, by whom the honors of the senate are sought after only as means of obtaining notice in the courts.

" The labors of a representative who is sedulous in the discharge of his duty are numerous and burdensome.

" It is neither just, nor reasonable, nor safe, that they should continue to be gratuitously rendered.

" We demand that in the future election of members of your Honorable House the approbation of the constituency shall be the sole qualification; and that to every representative so chosen shall be assigned, out of the public taxes, a fair and adequate remuneration for the time which he is called upon to devote to the public service.

" Finally, we would most earnestly impress on your Honorable House that this petition has not been dictated by any idle love of change; that it springs out of no inconsiderate attachment to fanciful theories; but that it is the result of much and long deliberation and of convictions, which the events of each succeeding year tend more and more to strengthen.

" The management of this mighty kingdom has hitherto been a subject for contending factions to try their selfish experiments upon.

" We have felt the consequences in our sorrowful experience—short glimmerings of uncertain enjoyment swallowed up by long and dark seasons of suffering.

" If the self-government of the people should not remove their distresses, it will at least remove their repinings.

" Universal suffrage will, and it alone can, bring true and lasting peace to the nation; we firmly believe that it will also bring prosperity.

" May it, therefore, please your Honorable House to take this our petition into your most serious consideration; and to use your utmost endeavors, by all constitutional means, to have a law passed granting to every male of lawful age, sane mind, and unconvicted of crime the right of voting for members of

Parliament; and directing all future elections of members of
Parliament to be in the way of secret ballot; and ordaining
that the duration of Parliaments so chosen shall in no case
exceed one year; and abolishing all property qualifications in
the members; and providing for their due remuneration while
in attendance on their Parliamentary duties.

" And your petitioners, &c."

APPENDIX D

A DIALOGUE ON WAR, BETWEEN A "MORAL FORCE" WHIG,
AND A CHARTIST, BY BRONTERRE [1]

QUID NUNC: Well, Bronterre, so we are going to *have*
a war *at last*.

BRONTERRE: To have a war! You talk of war as if it were
a possession, an acquisition, or a *means* of acquisition. But
how do you know we are going to *have* a war?

QUID NUNC: Why, all the newspapers say so; but you, it
seems, don't like war.

BRONTERRE: Don't like war! Why the deuce should I like
war? Why should I like murder and robbery, for murder
and robbery's sake; and what is war but murder and robbery?
But whom are we going to war with?

QUID NUNC: Ah! that is not yet decided on. It may be
with Russia, or with Canada, or with France, or for that
matter, with all three. I only wish it may be with some of
them, and soon: for allow me to say, I think differently of
war from what you do. Wars are often just and necessary;
or why be at the expense of maintaining fleets and armies?
Besides, a war is wanted just now, to give a *stir*, a *fillip*, a
new *impetus* to the country. We never had such prosperity
as during the American and French wars. Can you deny that?

BRONTERRE: You perfectly astonish me! You who pro-
fess to be a thorough-going liberal,—a moral force man,—
a march of intellect man,—a greatest happiness principle man,
and so forth, *you!* to talk thus of *war*, as if it were mere pastime, or a mere paltry commercial question of pounds, shill-

[1] *McDowall's Chartist and Republican Journal*, nos. 21 and 22, 1841.

ings and pence. Hang me, my good friend, if I can at all
comprehend your slaughtering *liberality*. As for the broken
arms and broken legs—the bursting of bombs scattering death
all around—the sacking and burning of whole towns and
villages, and ravishing of wives and virgin daughters—whole
fields strewn with dead bodies—hospitals crowded with agon-
ized and dying wretches, and their hardly less wretched sur-
vivors, exposed to every imaginable hardship and privation—
exposed to the war of elements as well as the war of bombs
and muskets—and often obliged to feed on cats, rats, and
stinking horse-flesh; and as for these and the like pretty
incidents of war, they evidently form no item of your profit-
and-loss account. You are too *liberal*, I suppose, or too much
a man of the world to regard trifles of that sort, more especially as you can afford to keep your own carcase out of the
way of the howitzers. But tell me, my good friend, how it
happens, that you, being a disciple and admirer of Joseph
Hume, make no distinction between fighting against Canada,
and fighting against France or Russia? Do you mean to say
it is quite indifferent to you with whom we go to war, provided only that we give a " new fillip or impetus to the country? " Do you—

QUID NUNC: Are you done?

BRONTERRE: Go on.

QUID NUNC: By jingo, Bronterre, if I did not know you so
well, and if you did not use " hell " and the " devil " so often,
I should almost fancy you to be a Quaker, you have such a
pious horror of war. But what use is there railing at what
neither you nor I can prevent? There cannot be war, of
course, without killing and wounding, but as there were wars
before you and I were born, so believe me, there will be wars
after you and I are dead. Now for your question, (and mind
that you answer mine in turn), you ask why I, a liberal, make
no distinction between fighting against Canada, and fighting
against France and Russia? I *do* make a distinction. On
political grounds, I should be sorry to see a war against the

Canadian insurgents, because I approve their cause; but I desire one on my brother's account, who being a saddler and harness maker, had recently a Government contract for the supply of saddles and harness for our Canadian troops, and who is promised another job or two if the war goes on. Now, having frankly answered your question, do you as frankly answer me those three: 1st. If our Indian possessions be attacked by Russian intrigue and Russian arms, is it not your duty, and the duty of all true patriots to assist in defending them, and *by war*, if necessary? 2nd. If our Mexican trade be similarly endangered by France, or our Mediterranean trade by the same power, are we not similarly justified in defending both against France, and *by war*, if necessary? 3rd. If, in both these cases, you disapprove of war, in what case would you approve of it; or would you, in all possible cases, and under all circumstances, dissuade the working classes from participating in war? No declamation, now! But straightforward answers.

BRONTERRE: Well, then, I shall be as frank as you have been. To your first question I reply,—Let all who have possessions in India, or all who profit by what you call our " Indian *possessions* ", be off to India, and fight a thousand battles for them, if they like. Let the proprietors of the East India Stock, let the owners of ¬ast India merchantmen, let those English and Irish merchants and brokers, and writers and underwriters, and governors and judges, and naval and military officers, and liver-¬olored nabobs, and all such other aristocrats and commercial speculators as have either wrung, or are now wringing, fortunes out of Hindoo sweat and misery—let all such persons go and fight for our " *Indian possessions* ", but let them not mock our degradation by asking us, working people, to fight along with them, either for our " *possessions* " in India, or anywhere else, seeing that we do not possess a single acre of ground, or any other description of property in *our own country*, much less colonies, or " possessions ", in any other, having been robbed of everything we

ever earned, by the upper and middle classes. Let the parties
I have described go and fight their own battles against Russia,
who, for all we care, may seize "*our Indian possessions*"
tomorrow if she likes. We, the working people of Great
Britain and Ireland, have no interest whatever in defending
those "possessions", nor any colonial possessions, nor any
other description of possessions belonging to men who have
robbed us of our political rights and franchises. On the contrary, we have an interest in prospective loss or ruin of all
such "*possessions*", seeing they are but instruments of power
in the hands of our domestic oppressors. Yes, yes, by all
means, let Russia seize them, if she can, and we shall but
thank God and Russia for the seizure.

To your 2nd question, my reply is—I care not how soon
France engrosses or destroys "*our Mexican trade*", nor to
what extent her Algerine conquests may operate to the prejudice of our commerce in the Levant or elsewhere. I should
rather see the whole of that commerce utterly extinguished,
than see one solitary working man lose a leg or an arm, in
war, to defend it. As commerce is now conducted, it is not
only without profit, but it is absolutely ruinous to the pro-
ductive classes of this country. When England had hardly
any foreign commerce at all, (in the year 1495), an English
laborer's weekly wages would buy 199 pints of wheat, and an
artisan's weekly wages 292 pints of wheat. We have now
more foreign trade than any other three nations in the world,
and, at least one hundred times more of it than we had in
1495; yet an English laborer's weekly wages will not bring
him, in this present year, more than 80 or 90 pints of wheat,
and an artisan's hardly 150 pints; not to speak of the difficulty
of getting employment,—a difficulty unknown in 1495. Talk
of our foreign trade, indeed! And fighting for it, too! Let
those who profit by it go and fight for it. Let the merchants
and shipowners, and big manufacturers and capitalists, who
gain rapid fortunes by it, let these persons go and fight for it.
Or let our aristocracy, to whom it brings tropical fruits, and
oriental perfumes, and rich furs and cashmeres, and pearls

and pieces, and shells and turtle, and delicious wines, and cordials, and ivory and lace, and silks and satins, and turkey carpets, and Chinese ornaments, and birds of paradise, *etc., etc.*, let these parties go and fight for it. To us, the working people, it brings next to nothing in exchange for the forty or fifty millions' worth of goods we are every year sending abroad. The only commodities the working class want from abroad are necessaries, and these are excluded by our Corn Laws. No, no, Mr. Quid Nunc! If Englishmen are to fight now-a-days, it must be for something better than you imagine. But no fighting for " our foreign trade "! No fighting for it at any rate until we have obtained our political rights and reformed our commercial system. I am no enemy of commerce, if commerce means what it ought to mean; but perdition, eternal perdition to the system which, under that name, is now impoverishing and brutalising the largest and best part of the human family.

To your 3d question my reply is—I have so inveterate and mortal an antipathy to *war* (regarding it as but another name for murder and robbery on a large scale), that only the direst necessity could induce me to be, under any circumstances, its advocate; yet, there is one great barbarous Power in Europe against which I should gladly see a war got up even this very day.

QUID NUNC: You mean Russia?

BRONTERRE: Softly, my good Sir. I mean a power more barbarous and barbarising than all other living despotisms put together, that of Russia included.

QUID NUNC: By the ghost of Nicholas! that is impossible; but name it.

BRONTERRE: I will neither name it nor describe it. You being a disciple of Hume and Grote, and I being the very antipodes of that school, we cannot possibly understand one another. Were I simply to *name* it—you would laugh outright, and to *describe* it I am incapable. But, as I perceive

your curiosity is on the rack I will leave a copy of the last
week's *Northern Liberator*, and from its leading article you
may possibly be able to form some faint idea of the power I
allude to.   Farewell!

* * *

The article referred to describes the English ruling classes
as "more despotic than despotism." Enumerating the evil
effects of the Corn Laws, the New Poor Law, the factory
system, the lack of universal suffrage, and the like, Bronterre
concludes his philippic in his characteristic style:

Could despotism do more than fill the country with starvation, poverty, tears, and blood; could despotism do more than
cover it with prisons, police houses, correction houses, penitentiaries, and Poor Law bastiles, where cruelties the most
atrocious and crimes the most *unnatural* are perpetrated upon
the wretched people by the horrid officials of these dens; could
despotism the most devilish do more than treat a people thus,
and then systematically refuse to listen to their complaints,
and treat their tears with menaces and their cries with abusive
calamities; in short, could the despotism of Nero, Tiberius,
Helagabalus and Herod, joined in one, do more than invert
and remorselessly carry into execution such a system *as now
exists in England!* . . . Men of England, and of Scotland,
and of Ireland! will you ever again shed your blood in defence of such a system? If you do, you deserve more than
you have already suffered.   But I wrong you by the question.
I forget, at the moment, that by recent demonstrations in favor
of Chartism you had virtually sealed the doom of that system.
Your long and bloody anti-Jacobin war against France was
the last you will ever engage in to uphold exclusive government.   Henceforth if you go to war, it shall be to fight *for
yourselves. No more anti-Jacobin wars! No coalition ministry!* No Tory-strong government! That's the ticket.

INDEX

VITA

The author of this monograph was born May 11, 1882, in Volhynia, Russia. The son of a Hebrew scholar, he was taught Hebrew, Talmud and the rabbinical literature up to the age of fourteen. He was then allowed to take up a course in a Russian classical gymnasium. In the Spring of 1903, he emigrated to Switzerland and from there, in September of the same year, to the United States. In 1906 he was admitted as a senior student to Columbia College and, upon his graduation in 1907 with the degree of A. B., registered under the Faculty of Political Science of Columbia University, choosing Economics as a major and Sociology and Philosophy as minors. He received the degree of A.M. in 1908. In 1907 and 1908 he was awarded University Scholarships in the Department of Economics. In his postgraduate studies he took courses with Professors Seligman, John B. Clark, Seager, Giddings, H. L. Moore, Simkhovitch, Mussey, Dewey, Montague, and others and attended the Seminar in Economics. In 1909 he was employed by the National Monetary Commission. From October, 1910, to February, 1912, he was connected with the work of the Tariff Board in Washington, D. C. He then held the position of Expert Special Agent with the New York State Department of Labor until September, 1914, when he accepted the office of general secretary and executive director of a fraternal death and sick benefit insurance corporation.

Milton Keynes UK
Ingram Content Group UK Ltd.
UKHW020723120923
428521UK00006B/357